# WARBIRDS IN THE CLOAK OF DARKNESS

©2018 Sandra Fabian Butalla

Published by Hellgate Press

(An imprint of L&R Publishing, LLC)

Hellgate Press
PO Box 3531
Ashland, OR 97520
*email*: info@hellgatepress.com

*Cover & Interior Design*: L. Redding

Cataloging In Publication Data is available from the publisher upon request.

*ISBN: 978-1-55571-921-0 (paperback)*

*ISBN: 978-1-55571-922-7 (ebook)*

Printed and bound in the United States of America

First edition 10 9 8 7 6 5 4

*This book is dedicated to Robert Eugene Holmstrom and his family, to Eleanor and Louis J. Fabian...and to Janice and Randy Wallake; Derek and Barb Olson; Erika, Brian, Wyatt, and Lane Kneen; Karen Silverwood; Ragan; and Jack for their support.*

# Contents

# Acknowledgments

MUCH CREDIT IS DUE TO Janice Wallake, without whose encouragement this story would never have been told. It was she who met Brian Grams, whose father John Grams lead me to Robert Eugene Holmstrom. As always, it was Jan who supported me  every step of the way in producing this book. And my deep appreciation goes to her daughter Ragan Wallake, for the gift of a laptop computer that was invaluable for my remote access to the developing manuscript in creating this book.

A good deal of credit must also be given to Robert Holmstrom's devoted daughter, Jennifer Nelson. She supplied several DVDs, a wealth of information regarding the Carpetbaggers, and all of the original photographs portrayed in this book.

Valuable assistance was provided by the Lakes Public Library in Fort Myers, Florida. Thanks to Manager Jill Horom and the entire reference staff for help in the use of their wonderful facility.

A debt of gratitude is owed to Kylie, Carlos, and Vincent from Microsoft, and to Dustin Miller from Tech Bytes in Eveleth, Minnesota, for their invaluable technical assistance.

Finally, my heartfelt thanks to Harley Patrick at Hellgate Press for his wisdom, advice, and infinite patience, and to the staff who helped to create and publish this book.

# Author's Note

THE PRIMARY INSPIRATION FOR ME IN writing this book was the pride and joy I have experienced since my first book, *The Man Who Fell to Earth* was published in 2016. Friends and family of Robert Givens, the World War II veteran whose incredible story made that book a success, have expressed a deep appreciation for the experience of reading it, and the honor it has brought to Bob Givens. I was able to read the manuscript to Bob before he passed away. He was thrilled to know that his life story was being preserved for his family and for posterity.

A year later, I learned of another World War II veteran who had a unique experience during the war, unlike most others. He was part of a highly-classified group of flyers who had been carefully selected to perform extremely dangerous missions. They were sworn to secrecy during the war while performing these missions and for an additional forty years after the war ended.

Once more it's another "Bob." This man is Robert Holmstrom, and this amazing story has long been a secret. I was thus compelled to create this book and lift the veil of secrecy that surrounded the truth of what some of our young men were doing to preserve our freedom and that of many other countries as well. While more than forty years have passed since the end of World War II, most of the men involved in these covert operations have remained silent about their involvement, even though it has been declassified. Few of them are alive today, and few people have any knowledge of their part in the heroic missions that saved many lives and helped considerably to win that horrible war.

And so, I embarked upon another long journey into the inspiring life experience of another "Bob." Now I look forward to sharing his story with you.

This book contains a compilation of historical events in connection to the people who were instrumental in them. The information for these events and the biographical portrayals of the people involved were drawn from a variety of sources, including organizations, internet, military magazines, and books. Primary book sources for which much of the invaluable factual and historical content presented in this book include:

-Conant, Jennet. *A Covert Affair*. New York: Simon and Schuster, 2011.

-Kindersley, Dorling. *Smithsonian WWII*. New York: DK Publishing, 2015.

-McKay, Sinclair. *The Secret Lives of Codebreakers*. New York: Penguin Group, 2010.

-Persico, Joseph E. *Roosevelt's Secret War*. New York: Random House Inc., 2001.

-Waller, Douglas. *Wild Bill Donovan*. New York: Free Press, 2011.

In addition, the events in the life of Robert Holmstrom as they appear in this book are as he himself recalled them. Any departure from the truth or actual facts by either Robert Holmstrom or myself is purely unintentional.

—*S. Fabian Butalla, 2018*

# Introduction

## 1944

A FOREST ON THE EASTERN BORDER OF GERMANY. A man embraces the trunk of a tree as he stands shuddering in the cool night air. Darkness has woven its fingers throughout the thick woods and he has reason to be fearful. He arrived at this place more than an hour ago and he has not moved since then. His breath comes in short, shallow spurts as he waits. He has been here before and he has waited before, for the moon to rise. The first glimpse is a hint of amber on the horizon. As minutes pass, a yellow arc grows slowly into a golden orb that continues to rise in the dark sky. The gold turns to silver, and as the moon continues its steady ascent in the night sky, shafts of light penetrate the blackness between the trees, revealing a secret – there are others in the forest. There are both men and women, as well as some older children, all waiting for something…and they wait at great peril to themselves.

They cannot see it, but they all hear it. From afar, a faint sound is detected—a sound they all recognize. At first it is merely a purr, but it morphs into a steady drone as it gets nearer. Finally, it is a deafening rumble as it approaches, and there it is—a huge B-24, painted entirely black, flying low with no lights over the tree tops. It has come to deliver its load, which in this case is not a bomb. Rather, it is the highly-anticipated supplies desperately needed by these people of the resistance against Hitler's Nazi regime.

The plane has something else to deliver—spies. These were highly- covert missions flown by a group of specially-trained U.S. airmen, who were code-named "Carpetbaggers." The men and women (some spies were female,) and those on the ground, all participated in the dangerous air drops into enemy territory, acknowledging the risk to themselves.

These secret, extremely dangerous missions were carried out by a select group of World War II airmen and women who were there in response to the people waiting in the forest. The plane's crew of "Carpetbaggers" shielded the reality of America's involvement in clandestine operations during the war. They were sworn to secrecy for forty years after the war ended.

It has become one of America's best-kept secrets.

# WARBIRDS IN THE CLOAK OF DARKNESS

The Amazing True Story of American Airman
Robert Holmstrom and the Top Secret
'Operation Carpetbagger' During WWII

## S. FABIAN BUTALLA

HELLGATE PRESS     ASHLAND, OREGON

# 1

# Along the Shores
# of Gitchee Gumee

A YOUNG BOY SAT WITH HIS DOG ON A promontory high above the big lake. The wind fiercely blew the hair out of his eyes as it simultaneously forced large waves to collide with the rocky shoreline. As always, the boy was mesmerized by the unceasing cadence of the rolling water capped with white froth. Its collision with the shore was both thunderous and spectacular. Like an orchestra repeating the same chorus again and again, the waves continued the forceful march to their destiny on the rocks, culminating with a roar as a sudden explosion of water was hurled into the air. The little terrier barked loudly each time this happened, and the boy clapped, hoping for an encore, which was assured on that windy day.

The boy was Robert Holmstrom, called "Bob" or "Bud" by his family and friends. He and his dog named "Spot" often went to that same place, and he was spell-bound by the sight of the seemingly endless body of water, until his trance was broken by

The Great Lakes

the pain and growling in his stomach. Hunger was part of his everyday state-of-being. Slowly he stood and urged Spot to follow him to their home in Knife River, as they turned away from the huge lake known as "Superior," or "Gitche Gumee" (the "shining big-sea water" to the native American Ojibwe people).

Connected to the Atlantic Ocean by means of the St. Lawrence Seaway, the Great Lakes of the United States spread into the heartland of the North American continent. Furthest inland, and largest of the five lakes, is Superior, which borders Canada to the north, Wisconsin and Michigan to the south, and Minnesota to the west. According to *Lake Superior Magazine*, Superior is by surface area the world's largest fresh water lake (roughly the size of the state of Maine.)[1] At the westernmost point of this great lake is Duluth, Minnesota. Twenty miles from Duluth, up the north shore of the lake, lies the community of Knife River.

Around the turn of the century, many people from European countries emigrated to the United States in search of a better living. Groups of Scandinavians settled in the areas of northern

Minnesota to work in the iron ore mines or to cultivate farms, or to do any other kind of work they could find to support themselves and their families. They were particularly attracted to the landscape in this area since it was remarkably similar to their homeland with its forests, and its clear-water lakes and streams.

One of these men was named Uno Holmstrom, whose father had been born in Finland and emigrated to the U.S. with hopes of working in the iron ore mines around the town of Two Harbors, Minnesota. Uno worked as a laborer, doing any odd jobs that came his way. He met a girl named Goldie who had moved to the Knife River area, north of Two Harbors, after having traveled there by covered wagon with her family from Missouri. Along the way, her mother gave birth to a boy.

Uno and Goldie were married and on January 4, 1926, they traveled to the hospital in Two Harbors where they had a son and

The northern Minnesota home of Bob's maternal grandparents, where he spent his early years.

they named him "Robert Eugene Holmstrom." It was a bitter fifty degrees below zero that day. They moved frequently, with Uno seeking work wherever he could find it. For a few years Uno was hired to work on the construction of Highways 23 and 61, which is the north shore highway that runs from Duluth, Minnesota along the western edge of Lake Superior all the way to Thunder Bay, Canada. At times, Uno moved his family along with the construction crews.

Life was difficult for the young family, as they struggled to make ends meet. They basically lived off the land, with vegetables raised in a garden if they were in one place long enough to reap the harvest. Squirrels, fish, and rabbits were a staple of their diet, and the plentiful deer provided a valuable addition to their table if Uno had time to hunt, which was rare. They raised a few chickens and geese, which was a special treat when roasted. Goldie and her mother picked wild berries when they were in season, and everyone enjoyed them. Still there never seemed enough to satisfy the hunger of a growing boy, since much of what they were able to obtain had to be preserved for the days and months ahead.

As young Bob sensed it was dinnertime, he left the scenic overlook above Lake Superior, shouting, "Let's go, boy!" and Spot sprinted ahead as they returned to the rented farmhouse where the family was preparing to eat the evening meal. Three rabbits had been skinned and stewed with carrots, onions, and a few potatoes from the garden. The enticing aroma of cooked meat beckoned everyone to the table, yet it was a meager meal for five people. Bob and his parents had been living with his grandparents since he was born.

The largest pieces of meat were unquestionably delivered to the bowls of his grandfather and father. His mother and grandmother helped themselves next, with the remaining small pieces placed in Bob's bowl. Spot relished the occasional tidbit handed to him under the table by the boy. No one was full after the meal. At times, his uncle and his cousins would join them for dinner and they would bring extra food – often fish or birds.

It was a well-ingrained rule from early childhood in the Holmstrom household that only adults were allowed to speak at the table. Children were to remain silent until excused to leave the dining area. Any time Bob broke that rule or any other of his father's expectations, he was subjected to physical punishment. Uno Holmstrom was a hardened disciplinarian who believed in the old adage of "Spare the rod, spoil the child." Consequently, Bob was often the victim of a leather strap, then sent to bed.

His parents provided the basic needs for their son (food, clothing, and shelter,) but they neglected to give him the one thing that he both needed and craved, and that was love. Taking care of him was simply treated as part of their daily chores, and he was denied any show of affection.

Bob's only understanding of real love and devotion was nurtured in his early years by his relationship with Spot, who seemed to always sense his loneliness and pain as he followed him to his room after a whipping. The loyal little terrier would nestle closely to Bob, whimpering softly with compassionate eyes as the young boy cried himself to sleep again, sometimes not even knowing what he had done to deserve the punishment. Equal to the physical sting of the strap was the humiliation of being exiled to his sparsely-furnished room.

In spite of the treatment by his parents, Bob enjoyed living in that beautiful part of the country. The scenic water of the Knife River flowed across the road from the farmhouse where he spent his early years. During times of dry weather, the dark granite and basalt rocks of the riverbed were exposed. With plentiful rainfall, the river channeled a current of water that flowed between the cities of Two Harbors and Duluth on the way to its union with Lake Superior. The area was heavily forested. During the warmer months, meadows were graced with a profusion of brilliant wildflowers. Carpeting the spaces between the meadows and the woods were fields that were plowed and planted by farmers. They hoped for a harvest of crops to be consumed by their families and their farm animals.

Bob would tell you, "We were dirt poor, but I didn't know it." One summer, as the road crew moved further away from Two Harbors, Uno, Goldie, and their young son lived for the entire summer in a tent by a ditch along the highway. There was a dirt floor in the tent, that they covered with cardboard at night before lying down to sleep. Meals were cooked over an open campfire and clothes were washed in the river. A few others who could not find or afford to rent places to live, pitched tents near the Holmstroms. Bob just felt like they were on an extended camping trip and does not remember being uncomfortable in the tent – except for the multitude of mosquitos, which made you miserable as long as you were awake.

About the time Bob turned five years old, he had experienced many adventures with Spot and sometimes his cousins in that rugged terrain. It was not a happy day for him when his parents announced that they were moving because his father had heard about a better job. It didn't take long for them to get their meager possessions ready for the move. They headed more than 180 miles south to the metropolitan city of St. Paul, Minnesota, where Fort Snelling is located. From that fort, Bob Holmstrom would one day begin his clandestine military service in a second global war.

# 2

# Between Two Wars

E IGHT YEARS BEFORE BOB HOLMSTROM was born, "The War to End All Wars" was over. Throughout the ravages of World War I, nine million soldiers had died and twenty-one million had been wounded. An additional five million civilians had perished from starvation or disease.[1] Three international measures were taken in hopes of maintaining peace in the world:

1. First the Treaty of Versailles was signed in 1919 by the allied and associated powers and by Germany as an end of the unprecedented carnage.

2. The following year, the League of Nations was created in an attempt to prevent future devastation between countries. Headquartered in Geneva, Switzerland, it provided a forum for resolving international disputes, which would hopefully provide "security and a lasting, friendly peace."

3. Nine years later, with unrest in some countries around the world, a peace pact was proposed by Aristide Briand, French Minister of Foreign Affairs and developed by U.S. Secretary of State Frank S. Kellogg. It was signed in Paris on August 27, 1928.

Named the Kellogg-Briand Pact, it outlawed war as national policy. As with the League of Nations, it called upon those who signed it to settle their disputes in a peaceful manner. Countries who originally signed the pact included France, the United States, the United Kingdom, Ireland, Canada, Australia, New Zealand, South Africa, India, Belgium, Poland, Czechoslovakia, Germany, Italy, and Japan. Later, an additional forty-seven nations also signed, which ultimately made it a peace agreement between nearly all of the established nations of the world.[2]

All seemed well.

However, both the Kellogg-Briand Pact and the League of Nations faced the same problem. There was no way to enforce the regulations against those who broke them. In 1931, Japan attacked Manchuria. The Chinese were unprepared for such an act, and in a matter of a few months Japan had seized control of the entire region in the far north-eastern provinces of China, along with its valuable resources.[3]

Due to the world-wide Depression, no action was taken against the aggressor, and without interference, soon Japan occupied all of Manchuria, in clear violation of the Pact. In 1933 the Japanese delegates walked out of the League of Nations Council and never looked back. They continued their aggression into Chinese territories.[4]

As history has proven, several leaders around the world shared a lust for more land and power, which would splinter the pacts and treaties that had been signed with the intention of world peace.

1. Benito Mussolini became the dictator of Italy in 1925 after he successfully established a system of public works. As a result, when employment rose he gained popularity. However, his desire to enlarge his empire would eventually lead him down a path of shame and ruin.[5]

2. Showa Hirohito became emperor of Japan in 1926. He and

the people of Japan ascribed to the centuries-old belief that all of the Japanese emperors were descendants of the founding god. It was therefore the duty of the emperor to maintain the prosperity of the country. They also believed that "the Japanese were a superior race, destined to rule the world."[6]. Thus, they set their sights on China, rich in the natural resources that Japan lacked.

3. Joseph Stalin was appointed sole dictator of the Soviet Union on January 1, 1929. He began a long and vicious reign of terror against anyone who opposed him, and he became a heartless dictator, killing millions as he seized Ukrainian farmlands."[7]

4. Adolph Hitler, was to become Fuhrer of Germany in 1934. He had been nurturing the conviction that it was imperative for Germany to expand its "living space" for pure-bred German people, called "Aryans." By convincing the native Germans that all Jewish people were a threat to them, he would reduce the population in his country by many millions. He was just beginning to build the infamous "Nazi killing machine."[8]

Mussolini, Hirohito, Stalin, and Hitler—each of these leaders was convinced that he must expand his realm in order to secure power and prosperity. They vowed to let nothing stand in their way, including the Treaty of Versailles, the League of Nations and the Kellogg-Briand Pact, as they marched forward to inevitable war and even more death and destruction.

The only exception was the Japanese Emperor Hirohito, who remained passive in preventing the millions of deaths and devastation caused by his country's dominant Imperial Army.

The seeds of war were sown with Mussolini in Italy, Hirohito in Japan, Stalin in the Soviet Union, and Hitler in Germany, all with a strong desire to conquer other lands. Wars were but a matter of time on both sides of the world from countries in the western Pacific to those east of the Atlantic.

In the middle was the United States, recovering from World

War I. The U.S. had taken a firm position of neutrality. The vast majority of American citizens were strongly opposed to engaging in another war.

The situations in the Asian Pacific and in many European countries were becoming more threatening, although at that time, nearly everyone in the United States (including most of the leaders) failed to recognize it.

# 3

# The American
# Home Front

F RANKLIN DELANO ROOSEVELT WAS APPOINTED Assistant
Secretary of the Navy by President Woodrow Wilson. As
part of the Office of Naval Intelligence (ONI), in 1918, he
boarded the USS *Dyer*, the Navy's newest destroyer, and sailed
to the UK to witness war in Europe. He was "dazzled" by the
British espionage as he was warmly welcomed into their inner
sanctum by Admiral Sir Reginald "Blinker" Hall, who had created
the Royal Navy's code-breaking division called "Room 40."[1]

In 1921, Franklin Roosevelt was struck with polio, which cost
him the use of his legs, jeopardizing his future political career,
and crushing his ego as an avid athlete and strong man. Over
time, he was resigned to being a victim of the disease and he
taught himself to walk short distances in his braces. He was
careful not to be seen in public using his wheelchair.[2]

Many Americans had been enjoying the high life of the
Roaring Twenties when the economy began to splinter. As the
months went by, Americans became concerned. The downturn

accelerated, and Americans became fearful. According to one source, "On October 24, 1929, the stock market crash took place. Prices plummeted while volumes skyrocketed. Americans started to panic. The Dow Jones Industrial Average dropped twenty-five percent in four days. The stock market collapsed completely on October 29, 1929, and Americans, as well as people in other countries, were devastated. Within two weeks, more than the total cost of World War I had been wiped out.[3] "Many Americans lost their confidence in business along with losing their wealth and sense of well-being. The U.S. Stock Market crash heralded a depression that would last for a decade and affect many countries around the world."[4]

By 1930, Franklin Roosevelt sensed political opportunity. He began a campaign for the U.S. presidency, promoting government intervention in the economy to provide relief and reform. He projected a positive approach that helped him defeat Republican incumbent Herbert Hoover in November, 1932. By the time Franklin Delano Roosevelt took the office of President in March, 1933, there were thirteen million unemployed Americans, and hundreds of banks were closed. The United States had a new president; however, FDR, as he became commonly known, faced the greatest crisis in American history since the Civil War."[5]

****

A man named William J. Donovan had attended Columbia University, where he was a star on the football team, then graduated from Columbia Law School, where Franklin Delano Roosevelt was a classmate, but not a friend. In time, Donovan would be a star on "FDR's team," and together they would shape the future of America's secret intelligence.

In 1912, Donovan had joined the New York National Guard

as a captain and he became part of the 69th "Fighting Irish" Regiment. He was called into federal service in 1916 to assist in tracking down the Mexican bandit Pancho Villa.

Later in WWI, Donovan's regiment was again called into federal service, and he joined the 165th Regiment of the U.S. Army, also known as the "Rainbow Division" because of the cross-country makeup of its ranks. While leading the regiment, he ordered his men to perform extreme physical drills to prepare for battle, while also gaining their admiration for his "coolness and resourcefulness in battle" and for his persistent "never give up" attitude. Thus, he earned the title "Wild Bill," which followed him for the rest of his days, and he never failed to live up to it.

Donovan was wounded in action three times in World War I. By the end of the war, he had been promoted to colonel and was one of its most decorated soldiers.[6]

Following the war, Donovan established a Wall Street law firm and traveled a good deal to other countries for his corporate law clients and for pleasure. During these trips he met many leaders, including Benito Mussolini of Italy. Throughout his travels, Bill Donovan met many other influential people, and he made several important connections. He honed his skills as an intelligence gatherer overseas.[7]

Two young men from "opposite sides of the tracks" had ignored each other while attending Columbia Law School years before, but were soon to meet again. Although Franklin Delano Roosevelt and his former Columbia classmate, William J. Donovan, were affiliated with opposing political parties, they nonetheless had several things in common. They were both charismatic and determined, and both were fascinated by the secret world of international intelligence. Roosevelt respected Donovan's military experience and his global travels, along with the numerous connections he had cultivated. From his wheelchair, FDR envied

Donovan's passionate energy and his ability to travel everywhere in the world at the drop of a hat.

President Franklin Roosevelt had his eye on Bill Donovan for a future position that would prove to be "Wild Bill's" dream job.

# 4

# City Boy

I N THE FALL OF 1931, THE HOLMSTROM FAMILY moved to east St. Paul, Minnesota, where Bob was introduced to a whole new world. Far from the waters of Lake Superior, and the forest, river, and meadows he had known so well, the city was a complete change for him. Everyone and everything seemed to move faster. He needed to adjust and to do it quickly as he was enrolled in the first grade at Van Buren Elementary School. The boy had to walk three-quarters of a mile alone to and from the school each day. Once there, he was surrounded by more children than he had ever seen. Bob had been strictly disciplined at home, so he was accustomed to following rules and orders, and he was a bright boy, so he adapted rather quickly.

For the first time, Bob was introduced to sports, and he loved the group dynamics of playing on a team. Softball was his favorite because, as he said, "I was pretty good at it. I could really hit that ball."

On one Veterans Day, two World War I vets talked to the students about the war itself, their experiences in the war, and the sacrifices made by the men and women who were a part of it.

The presentation left a lasting impression on Bob, who had no prior knowledge of the war.

His family joined the First Lutheran Church of St. Paul, and new opportunities opened to Bob. There was another group of children and activities that he loved. The choir was something he was happy to join, and from that early age, he developed an ability to sing and read music.

Then there was Boy Scout Troop 101, which operated out of the church. This was one of the most positive influences in Bob's life. "Our leaders were exceptionally good. They taught us so much," he said. "They helped us to be able to express ourselves so others could understand, also how to be a leader, and to make ourselves presentable. We learned survival skills like how to tie different kinds of knots with rope, and to do it quickly and securely. We learned about basic first aid and how to treat burns and to splint broken bones. They taught us how to make something out of nothing, especially in the woods, such as how to make furniture to sit on and tying branches together for shelter. Making a fire with flint and steel was another lesson, and making it with sticks and small kindling was yet another. We were taught how to get water from condensation with a piece of plastic, what kind of berries were edible and when to pick them so you didn't get sick, and how to make tea from leaves. We also learned about certain roots you could boil and eat."

Then there were hunting skills that were learned, although Bob was already familiar with most of them from his early years up north. They made snares out of wire to catch rabbits and how to make a spear from a tree limb to catch fish. The boys were also introduced to astronomy in their study of the stars and how the sun and the constellations can help you to plot direction. Bob absorbed every bit of what the Scouts taught him and he was grateful for the experience.

There was a Fathers and Sons Club at the church and Bob's dad came a couple of times. One of those times was a big deal. A famous athlete was coming to talk to them, followed by a banquet. The athlete was Bronislau "Bronko" Nagurski, three-time National Football League champion who had an illustrious career playing for the Chicago Bears, while at the same time earning accolades as two-time National Wrestling Alliance World Heavyweight Champion in another great career as a professional wrestler. Bob and the others were impressed by his size (6'2", 226 pounds of highly-conditioned muscle,) and even more by his message: "You can do anything you want if you set your mind to it."[1] It was an important message Bob never forgot. The banquet that followed was great and Bob said, "I was really hungry!"

Bob was in the 4th grade, when his sister Carol was born. He was soon assigned the duties of babysitter on a regular basis whenever he was not in school or church. Then began a parade of homes for them as they moved frequently, seeking cheaper rent or a better location. The first of these moves took them only a half-block from the Van Buren School, so Bob's walk there was shortened. That same year he was forced to change to the Sibley Public School as they had moved again.

Their next move took them to an old apartment house. While he remembered the inside being "not too bad," outside there were rats. "It's a good thing we were on the second floor," Bob exclaimed, as he did not recollect seeing any in their apartment. His dad had the use of a truck for his job and it was difficult to start, so each morning Bob had to get up at five a.m. to help his dad push it down the hill in order to get it going. One good thing about living there was the proximity of his godmother's son, Gary. He and Bob would visit the neighborhood drug store where the owner would kindly allow the two boys to sit and read the comic books, then return them to the rack without paying, which they very much appreciated.

After the apartment, they moved into a house in a better part of town, where their neighbor owned a spaghetti restaurant. "He was really nice, and would sometimes give us spaghetti dinners. And he taught me a lot about how to raise tomatoes and other garden tips," said Bob. Between 1939 and 1940, Bob had to once more change schools and enroll in Harding High School. He was there for less than a year when they moved again.

This time, they were going back up north.

# 5

# Between the Rock
# and the Hard Spot

W HILE BOB HOLMSTROM WAS GROWING UP throughout the 1930s, America had persisted in remaining "neutral" in world affairs. The last thing American citizens wanted was to ever be involved in another war after the extraordinary destruction and the death and injury toll from World War I. Franklin Delano Roosevelt, U.S. President since 1933, had been doing his best to adhere to the policy of "isolationism." As a result, a blind eye was turned by the U.S. government to the Japanese occupation of Manchuria, Hitler's escalation of an enormous German arms buildup, Stalin's invasion of Poland and other countries, and Mussolini's invasion of Ethiopia by Italy.

The U.S. Congress passed a series of laws that banned the sale of arms and loans to countries at war as a means of removing any potential reason the United States may have for entering a conflict in Europe.

The world was shocked by the Japanese on December 13, 1937 with their invasion of China that came to be called "The Rape of

Nanking." It was a massacre of as many as 300,000 people, yet there was no U.S. response. Even when an American gunboat was sunk by the Japanese while transporting evacuees from Nanking, once again, the United States remained "neutral."[1]

In 1938, Winston Churchill urged an alliance between the U.S. and the USSR following the German invasion of the Sudetenland. Several days later, Roosevelt responded by stating that the United States would not join a "stop-Hitler movement" and it would remain neutral over the invasion of Czechoslovakia (Sudentenland).

FDR was caught between the "rock and the hard spot" in his perseverance to maintain the neutrality of the United States. After intense Congressional debate over the issues of neutrality vs. aid to the Allies, they eventually granted their approval to aid the Allies.

Roosevelt then faced a deeply divided nation between those who, like himself, believed that the aid would be sufficient to keep the U.S. out of the war, while the "isolationists" believed that his policies would lead the country into another disastrous war. The debate raged on.

# 6

# FDR Takes Action

I N 1939, EVENTS BEGAN HEATING UP and the United States was edging ever closer to becoming involved in what was to become World War Two.

In August, Albert Einstein told President Franklin Roosevelt that German physicists were engaged in uranium research. He further informed him about the German Atomic Energy Program and the importance of research in nuclear chain reactions and the possibility of creating powerful bombs.

Early on the morning of September 1, 1939, Franklin Roosevelt was informed that "Germany was attacking Poland with sixty divisions and more than a thousand aircraft!" Two days later, Britain gave Germany an ultimatum to leave Poland.

Then, on September 3, 1939, Britain and France declared war against Germany.

The President gathered his military advisors and members of Congress, after which a domino-effect of actions took place in order to protect the United States from attack:

• *September 8*: FDR proclaims a limited state of emergency in the U.S.

• *September 9*: FDR increases the strength of the U.S. Navy and Marine Corps and recalled active duty officers, men, and nurses on retired lists.

• *October 1*: The U.S. Navy now consists of 396 commissioned ships.

• *October 5*: The Hawaiian Detachment is formed and sent to its new operating base at Pearl Harbor.

• *November 4*: U.S. Congress modifies the Neutrality Act, allowing arms trade on a "cash and carry" basis, ending the arms embargo.

• *November 4*: U.S. contracts for atomic research with the Universities of Columbia, Chicago, and California.[1]

The year 1939 was also the year in which a device was finally unveiled that would change aerial warfare. A man named Carl van Norden was a Dutch engineer who had emigrated to the United States in 1904. By 1913 he became well known for his work with Elmer Sperry on the first "gyrostabilizing equipment" for U.S. ships. He had formed his own company in 1913 and started working on a bombsight, which is an instrument used to guide the trajectory of a bomb once it is released from a plane, directly toward its intended target. By 1920 he had begun work on the Norden bombsight for the U.S. Navy.

It was not until 1931, when the new bombsight was unveiled. It was described as "revolutionary," and the media of the day touted the claim that "bombadiers using the Norden bombsight could hit a pickle barrel from twenty thousand feet." Norden expounded on that claim by stating, "When better pickle barrels are built, Norden will hit them, too!"[2]

The Norden bombsight was highly classified and considered one of the country's "most valuable secrets." As a result, no photographs were allowed nor was any release of specifications or performance data to the public allowed. Washington developed an intricate, highly secure system for shipping and handling the Norden bombsight. The unit had to be covered except when in use, delivered to the aircraft by an escort of armed guards, and returned to specialized bombsight storage vaults between flights. Furthermore, there was even a "bombadier's oath," which pledged a person to kill oneself in the event of imminent capture. Additional regulations called for destroying the unit with a bullet, a blowtorch-like device, or ripping it out and throwing it overboard.[3]

Meanwhile, Britain, in spite of their advanced intelligence, did not possess a bombsight of this caliber, and Prime Minister Neville Chamberlain personally wrote to President Roosevelt, asking him to share the Norden bombsight with the British. Still leery of alienating the American isolationists, FDR refused, and even when Chamberlain offered to share radar technology, he once again declined.

Then, having ignored Einstein's letter for two months during which he was preoccupied with conflicts that were occurring in Europe, FDR was met by his longtime friend, Wall Street economist Alexander Sachs to discuss the letter and its implications. Sachs pointed out the downside of being left in the dust in this race to build a powerful bomb. Concerned about funding such expensive research, Roosevelt did not immediately commit to a plan to address the issue. However, he finally became convinced of the value of such an enterprise, and he enlisted the aid of the most brilliant refugee scientists and physicists who had emigrated to the U.S.

He responded to Einstein on October 19, 1939 by telling him that he had set up a committee with representatives from both the Army and the Navy to study uranium. It was the first of many steps toward the development of was to become known as "The

Manhattan Project." It would eventually lead to the development of the atomic bomb. Several research facilities from Tennessee to Washington to New Mexico and university laboratories from Columbia to Berkeley were involved. Secrecy was top priority in all facets of this research and in all facilities.[4] Franklin Delano Roosevelt went into high gear once he decided to act.

Many of the people who were employed for years at those facilities never knew exactly what it was they were working on.

# 7

# Helter Skelter

B Y 1939, MANY COUNTRIES AROUND THE WORLD were either invading others or fighting to resist invasion. The peace pacts and treaties they had signed were left in the dust. What follows is a partial timeline of events from late 1939 through late 1941:

•*September 1939*: War in Europe is declared. Germany and Russia have formed an alliance and both are in high gear by 1940. Germany invades Poland following the collapse of their army. Stalin orders the mass murder of twenty thousand Polish officers, soldiers, and civilian prisoners-of-war during what comes to be known as the infamous Katyn Forest Massacre. The Nazi army moves on to invade Norway and then occupy Denmark.

•*1939*: Across the Pacific, Japanese forces continue their invasions. They initiate the bombing of Chunking and gain the portions of China that are richest in natural resources.

•*1940*: the United States has been increasing its military buildup, and on May 9, President Roosevelt orders the entire U.S. Pacific fleet to Pearl Harbor, Hawaii. This is intended to be a

warning to Japan to cease their invasion of other territories. Japan
shows no interest in complying.

•*May 10, 1940*: Germany invades the Netherlands, Belgium,
and Luxembourg. Two days later, Hitler's army invades France
and "all hell breaks loose." One month later, the Nazis occupy
Paris, France.

•*June 1940*: Italy declares war on Britain and France while
Stalin's army invades Romania. Then Mussolini's forces move
into Africa and overtake cities in Sudan.

•*July 1940*: With no sign of Japan relenting its aggression,
FDR takes another step by ordering a ban on strategic materials
shipped to the country. Three weeks later, he places an embargo
on scrap metal and petroleum to Japan. The message was clear.
Five days later, the Battle of Britain (against Germany)
commences.

•*September 16, 1940*: The first peacetime draft of the U.S.
Selective Service begins as men aged 21-35 are called to duty.
Less than two weeks later, Japan, Germany, and Italy form the
Axis powers.

•*August - September 1940*: Mussolini's army invades Greece
and then Egypt.

•*January 1941*: Japan continues gathering U.S. intelligence
through a secret network.

•*April - May 1941*: Germany invades Yugoslavia and Crete.
Mussolini's army in eastern Africa is forced to surrender after
being defeated by the British, resulting in 300,000 casualties.

•*July 25, 1941*: The United States and the U.K. agree to freeze
Japanese assets. Three days later, Japan responds by freezing
U.S. assets.

•*Mid-October, 1941*: Japanese Prime Minister Hideki Tojo and
the Imperial Army strike forces begin conducting training
exercises.[1] Apparently, they had a plan.

# 8

# Country Boy

U NAWARE OF THE MILITARY CONFLICTS happening around
the world at that time, fourteen-year-old Bob Holmstrom
and his family had once again settled in northern
Minnesota. The "Iron Range" is an area of northeastern
Minnesota where an enormous deposit of iron ore (over one
hundred ten miles long, one to three miles wide, and in places,
as thick as five hundred feet) has been mined for more than one
hundred years.[1] The area borders the western shores of Lake
Superior roughly from Duluth north to Canada and west halfway
across the state.

When the Holmstrom family moved from St. Paul in 1940,
they headed back to that part of the state known as the Iron
Range. This time they settled seventy-three miles northwest of
Knife River, into a rustic cabin on Lake Eshquagama south of
Biwabik, Minnesota.

There was a wood stove in their living room, which they used
until the summer months, when it was carried out to a shed on
the edge of the property. In 1940, to the surprise of everyone there
that year, it snowed on the 4th of July. Bob and his father had to

carry the woodstove back into the cabin. Throughout the summer Bob caught "lots of bass" in the lake and he enjoyed the old sauna down by the water. He said, "I never got sick or had a cold because of it."

Once when his cousin visited, they were standing in chest-deep water. Bob did not know how to swim, so when his cousin playfully kicked his legs out from under him, Bob went underwater and panicked, sure he was going to die. Flailing around and swallowing a good amount of water, he somehow regained his footing and came up, gasping for breath. The lesson he learned was that he needed to teach himself another survival skill. He practiced all summer, dog-paddling between the dock in front of their cabin and the one next door, until he no longer had a fear of the water.

Sometimes Bob and his family would go to Two Harbors, north of Knife River, to visit his uncle Roy and his cousin Vernon, who had a .22 caliber rifle. His uncle taught Bob how to shoot the rifle and they hunted partridge and deer. He did not like shooting beaver, though, because "they had a real bad odor." Bob learned how to shoot at a target that was nothing more than a three-foot stick in the ground. Roy taught the boys how to stalk their prey, how to aim and shoot, and how to field-dress a deer or transport it back to the farm where it would hang on a hook for a while before it was skinned and cleaned out. Then the meat was cut up and packaged so it was ready for the "ice box." Bob learned many things from his uncle, who took the time to include him in the skills he was teaching his son. Many of these skills would be valuable in the years to come, particularly for Bob.

Occasionally the three of them would go fishing on Lake Superior in a sixteen-foot boat, trolling the waters between the Knife River and the French River, using rods with piano wire to catch lake trout, which were in deep water. Sometimes it was pretty rough and the outboard motor was not dependable, requiring many pulls to get it started.

His cousin liked to jump off a twenty-foot cliff into the lake and teased Bob into trying it once. He had taught himself how to swim by then, so after some anxious hesitation and the howls of the other boy, he ran toward the edge and plummeted through the air into the always-cold waters of Lake Superior. He could not get to the surface fast enough and was dealing with the shock of the frigid water, which literally sucked the breath out of him, while going into high gear with his best dog-paddle toward the shore. He said, "By the time you made it, you actually got used to the cold and it wasn't so bad."

What was bad was the fog on and along the area close to the lake. Bob remembered that, "On a clear day, you could see the Wisconsin shore twenty-six miles across the water. But if you were driving a car on a foggy day, many times someone else had to stand outside on the running board to see what was just ahead." The fog would roll across the waters of the great lake, and inch by inch, it would creep onto the shore as it enveloped the land beyond with its misty coolness and its silent secrets.

As fall approached, the Holmstroms moved into the town of Gilbert, Minnesota, where Bob was enrolled in Gilbert High School. Bob admitted that all of the moves they made during his childhood were "disturbing," as one can only imagine. "I tried really hard to learn, but it wasn't easy," he recalled. He did read a lot, especially about different countries and what was happening in the world. While at the Gilbert School, he played football. After every practice, Bob and several of his teammates were driven home by the coach in of all things—a Chrysler limousine, which he reckons was donated to the school by the local mining company.

Bob admits that "Christmas was the best time," but he never got any toys. He had to make his own toys like a scooter out of wooden planks from an apple crate mounted onto old roller skates. Otherwise, Christmas was the time he got "new" clothes. Actually, he never got anything new—just items that his mother had re-worked by turning the collar inside out or letting down the seam of a pair of pants. Goldie Holmstrom was an outstanding seamstress and could turn a rag into something presentable. With the use of an old sewing machine, she and her family appeared to be well-dressed, even with "hand-me-downs" and "cast-offs" from others.

Bob remembered one Christmas, however, that was different from all others. In 1936, his father had bought him a bicycle, but it was winter and Bob had to leave it in the basement until spring. When warmer weather arrived, his parents were short of cash and they had to sell the bike. Bob never had a chance to ride it.

While living in Biwabik, the house they rented had a "real good Zenith radio." Uno and Bob ran a copper wire from the barn to the house and they were actually able to listen to an English translation of Adolph Hitler addressing the Germans. "They were oppressed people and he promised them everything," Bob recalled.

It was the first time he had any idea of trouble brewing in Germany.

# 9

# The British Codebreakers

F IFTY MILES NORTH OF LONDON, IN Buckinghampshire, is the site of Bletchley Park, which was the highly-secret center for British codebreakers prior to and during World War II.[1] It was a hub of covert activity. People from a variety of backgrounds, including mathematicians, linguists and translators, and those skilled at chess and solving crossword puzzles would become part of a team of code-breakers. Many "Wrens" (Women's Royal Naval Service) were employed as clerks. The universities of Oxford and Cambridge provided many scholars, including Alan Turing, who was destined for fame with his code-breaking machine.[2]

On August 15, 1939, Bletchley Park became a training ground for cryptographers, otherwise known as "a Government Code and Cypher School," where members of the British Secret Intelligence (code-named "MI-6") occupied the top floor of the building. The demands on those who worked there were intense, but their country was in peril from German threats and the British people were proud to serve in this capacity for its security. There was a high level of secrecy surrounding all of the activities at Bletchley Park. Talking about any aspect of it was prohibited at meals, in travel, and even in their own homes.[3]

By 1940, the majority of those working at Bletchley Park were consumed with what was purported to be an impossible task. Using an electro-mechanical rotor cipher machine called the "Enigma," the Germans had developed a code that was ingenious. The greatest minds were put to the task of deciphering the code to no avail. It was the most perplexing puzzle imaginable because rotor scramblers were used and the primary keys to the code were changed daily, plus the mathematical configurations were infinite.[4]

As one source described it, "A basic Enigma machine could be set in several millions of ways and was regarded by both the Germans and the British as unbreakable."[5]

If the German radio messages could be decrypted, advance notice would be given to the British regarding the time and place of an impending attack by land, sea, or air, and it could change everything. However, it did not come without a price. With mounting unrest in Europe and the occupation by others of nearby countries, the British government had for years been increasing its military and did not have a monetary excess to put forth into funding years of attempted code-breaking.

Nonetheless, several brilliant people refused to give up on their attempts to break the "unbreakable code." Chief among the Bletchley codebreakers was Alan Turing, who fought vigorously to keep his experiments with Enigma alive. Threats of eliminating his research due to a lack of funding propelled him to work harder and faster. An engineer named Harold "Doc" Keen was able to "transform Turing's ideas into a working machine that replicated super-human brain activities of a human mind continuously dedicated to solving an extraordinarily complex puzzle."[6]

In the end, with the assistance of Harold "Doc" Keen, Alfred "Dilly" Knox, Gordon Welchman, and mathematicians John Jeffries and Peter Twinn, Alan Turing was successful. Their efforts saved millions of lives that would otherwise have been lost in World War II.

The "Turing machine" is now called a "computer."[7]

# 10

# FDR's Secret Weapon

B Y THE END OF JUNE IN 1939, President Roosevelt was increasingly frustrated with the duplication of information by the three major organizations who were commissioned to gather international intelligence. This included the Army's Military Intelligence Division (MID), the Office of Naval Intelligence (ONI), and the Federal Bureau of Investigation (FBI). Due to a serious rivalry among the three groups, there was a reluctance to share information. Rather, it became more of a race to become first to expose anything of significant importance. Therefore, on June 26th, FDR set up a meeting of the directors of intelligence in order to begin a synchronization of the three organizations. J. Edgar Hoover, chief of the FBI, failed to attend the meeting. It soon became obvious that he had no desire to share the power of his current position.[1]

On May 7, 1940, Prime Minister of the U.K. Neville Chamberlain resigned and Winston Churchill filled the vacancy.[2] Roosevelt and the new Prime Minister established a rapport and agreed to share some valuable military information. At the risk of jeopardizing America's policy of neutrality, FDR finally revealed information on the Norden bombsight, which had been actively sought after by Chamberlain, while Churchill shared information on British sonar (ADSIC).[3] This was a beneficial barter for both the United Kingdom and the United States and would serve them well in the years ahead.

What Roosevelt needed was an indomitable workhorse, someone who could accept the mantle of secrecy while performing the duties required of the head of an organization engaged in worldwide covert operations. It would not be a "cushy" assignment, but one that would require dedication, perseverance and stamina, as well as the ability and willingness to travel into the far corners of the world. There was one man who fit the bill perfectly, one man who seemed he was destined for this position. It was his former Columbia Law classmate, William J. Donovan.

FDR shared some traits with Donovan, who was commonly known as "Wild Bill." Both had an intense desire to serve their country. Both had long harbored a fascination with the clandestine. And Bill Donovan was a compulsive traveler who, as a business lawyer, had established important connections around the world in the last ten to fifteen years.

In 1939, Donovan traveled to Ethiopia to report back to FDR's administration on the Italian-Ethiopian War, Berlin, the Balkans and Italy, and he met with leaders in Belgium, Holland, and other countries.[4]

Donovan's reports and information were impressive and FDR was listening when Bill Donovan suggested that they begin a collaboration with British Intelligence by creating a centralized espionage service. Donovan believed Britain could survive a German attack if the United States offered the assistance for which Churchill had been pleading. Meanwhile, a British-U.S. secret liaison was needed. Again, William Donovan fit the bill better than anyone FDR knew at that time.

On July 14, 1940, at FDR's request, Wild Bill flew across the Atlantic on a clandestine trip as a civilian and entered the netherworld of espionage, that would consume the rest of his life.[5]

In the U.K., he met with Colonel Stewart Menzies, who was known as "C," the head of MI-6, Britain's Secret Intelligence Service. The British had many years of experience in the field of espionage, and "C" was eager to train Donovan, who was duly amazed with their sophisticated operation. While there, he also met Rear Admiral John Godfrey, head of British Naval Intelligence, and his naval aide, Commander Ian Fleming, who would one day fictionalize some of his own wartime experiences with his stories of the spy he called "James Bond—Agent 007.[6]

By the end of 1940, Donovan had convinced FDR to collaborate with the British as much as possible. So Roosevelt had a secret alliance with the U.K. and he had a secret weapon—Wild Bill Donovan!

# 11

# America's Spycraft

A HIGHLY MOTIVATED BILL DONOVAN RETURNED to Washington in 1941, where he laid the groundwork for a plan to get the United States up to speed with the world's major powers in the field of espionage. Armed with energy, ideas from the British Intelligence high command, and conviction, Wild Bill went all-out to convince Franklin Roosevelt that such an agency was a necessity – and it worked. FDR approved Donovan's proposal.[1] As a result of the high-powered delivery of Wild Bill's plan, Franklin Delano Roosevelt created America's first central intelligence agency.

After his remarkable display of due diligence, who should be named to that coveted position of "Coordinator of Intelligence (COI)" for the new agency? On July 11, 1941, Roosevelt created the post and with no competition, William J. Donovan readily accepted. He was to report only to the President.[2]

****

There is an age-old history of espionage in the world: the Bible tells of Moses sending twelve spies to the land of Canaan, George Washington sent spies to see if the French had penetrated British colonial soil, and Abraham Lincoln used the Pinkerton Detective Agency to spy for the Union, to name a few. Great Britain was the first to establish a permanent, publicly-funded spy service in 1909, followed by Germany, in 1913, Russia in 1917, and France in 1935.[3] The U.S., however, had none at the time.

Playing "catch-up" was going to be a daunting task for the new American COI. Not only did he enter the game late, but he faced resentment on the home front as well as with "allies." As a civilian, Donovan was rebuffed by other agencies, including the FBI and the joint Chiefs of Staff. Yet he persisted in his dedication to develop a central agency and overcame many obstacles thrown his way. Even the British, although they had urged collaboration, became wary of the notion of sharing too much information with the "American amateurs." Trust became an issue on both sides. However, Bill Donovan, true to form, forged ahead.[4]

President Franklin Roosevelt, on June 13, 1942, appointed William J. Donovan chief of the newly created Office of Strategic Services. The OSS was to be a centralized spy agency that would be tasked with gathering intelligence from sources overseas and reported directly to FDR. Bill Donovan went to work with his trademark gusto and began an immediate search for intelligent people to be employed on his staff. He believed "smart people can handle any job."[5]

Donovan had been in overdrive, as he set up training schools for agents at vacant Civilian Conservation Corps (CCC) camps, at National Parks in Maryland and Virginia, and on Santa Catalina Island, California. Donovan's advice to those who recruited potential agents was, "Hire on the spot anyone of great ability. Later we'll find out what they can do." As a result, "the OSS recruits came from a vast spectrum of civilian life, including journalists, linguists, explorers, traders, missionaries, scientists, etc. Secret agent training required a sixteen-week course where participants ultimately learned how to infiltrate defense plants, using false identities in an attempt to obtain secrets and to practice methods of deception in the event they were exposed."[6]

According to Jennet Conant, writing in her book titled *A Covert Affair,* "Secret agents were required to possess a very specific set of skills due to the dangerous nature of their assignments. They needed the ability to think quickly in order to imbed themselves in a different culture and environment, and they had to appear confident when facing danger. They were schooled in the culture and customs of the country to which they were assigned, and they had to possess at least a basic grasp of the language."[7]

She explains further that, "Agents were sworn to absolute secrecy regarding the nature of the OSS and their part in it. They were not to reveal anything about it to family or friends. They were admonished to guard their anonymity at all costs. Nothing that they carried personally was to reveal their true identity, because the one thing that was strictly forbidden was to blow cover."[8]

In case of capture, they carried an "L" (lethal) pill, which they were encouraged to use rather than to divulge any information pertaining to the OSS that could jeopardize their country's security. After completing their training, they were well-aware of the heavy responsibility and the inherent dangers they would bear. The thousands who accepted that burden were sent to far-fling countries around the world to collect and report intelligence to the OSS.

# 12

# The Big News Flash

U NO HOLMSTROM WAS A HARD WORKER, but the fact that he had to move his family back and forth so often in order to find jobs was "unsettling" to his teenage son Bob. They were living once again in St. Paul, Minnesota.

Bob naturally had a challenging time trying to adjust to so many changes in schools over the years and it was difficult to establish and maintain friendships as well. One boy named Bill was his most faithful friend over his years at Harding High School, where they participated on the basketball and track teams together. The First Lutheran Church in St. Paul became a center of fun and great satisfaction to Bob who, along with his family, attended three times a week. Bob's interest in classical music was nurtured by a part-time job he got serving as an usher at the St. Paul Auditorium. After everyone was seated, Bob was allowed to stay and enjoy the performances, and he was inspired.

He joined two choirs in his church including the Children's Choir and the Luther League Choir. He enjoyed both of them. They sponsored picnics, which were a welcome feast for the hungry young boys like Bob. The church also owned an island near Mille Lacs, Minnesota, where they had established a summer camp, which Bob was able to attend. It was fun to get away from the city and experience the outdoor life again.

While living on the east side of St. Paul, Bob was able to finally get a bicycle by obtaining parts and assembling them himself. Along with the Boy Scouts, he participated in bike trips, sometimes all the way to Hastings (eighteen miles away,) and they would stop to camp along the way and enjoy the famous "Boy Scout lunch," which consisted of baked beans and wieners cooked over an open fire. By the time it was done, the steamy contents smelled delicious and were devoured by most everyone, certainly by Bob Holmstrom. His family at that time lived close to a butcher shop, where they were able to get soup bones for free. "We ate a lot of soup," Bob admitted.

His mother Goldie was not the best cook. "She over-cooked everything," Bob said, "but she was a good baker. She was often a little sickly so I would run home from school around 11:00 a.m. and punch down the bread dough for her." He would run back to school and she would later put it in the oven. Then they would have fresh bread with their soup.

One of Bob's favorite pastimes while growing up was reading. He was becoming most interested in learning about other countries and what was happening there. His church hosted a missionary family who had worked with a Swahili tribe in Africa. Bob was intrigued and highly impressed with the program detailing their experiences there which they presented to the congregation. He tried to imagine the kinds of life others were living in faraway lands.

Then one day as Bob was sitting in church listening to the sermon which was about to end, someone rushed toward the pulpit, approached the minister, and whispered something in his ear.

With a shocked look on his face, the minister slowly made his way from the pulpit to the center of the communion rail, where he announced in a hoarse and quivering voice, "The Japanese have just attacked the U.S. fleet at Pearl Harbor!" Then he fell to the floor and passed out.

The congregation was duly stunned on that fateful day, December 7, 1941, as was everyone across America and the world. Communication was poor then. Most Americans had to wait for the radio news or cinema newsreels advising them of the horrific number of deaths, casualties, and sunken or otherwise destroyed ships and facilities in Pearl Harbor. Bob remarked that, "Many people didn't even know where Hawaii was, or Australia, or New Guinea. We knew we had to do something, but we didn't know what! We wondered what would happen if they attacked us here in the United States!"

He would have to wait a few years before he was able to join the military effort himself. Meanwhile, panic and pandemonium spread across the United States.

The U.S. had not wanted to get involved in other countries' conflicts. However, as Bob Holmstrom remarked, "On that day, out of the clear blue sky, we were involved!"

# 13

# Too Young to Serve

T HE MANY MOVES THE HOLMSTROM FAMILY made as Bob's father sought employment back and forth from northern Minnesota to numerous locations in St. Paul led his son in and out of several schools in the middle of sessions. It was a stroke of luck that Bob was intelligent and did so well in his studies where many others would likely fail under the circumstances. Instead, Bob learned how to adapt and he skipped from fifth to seventh grade. He felt he had received an excellent education while in the Iron Range schools. However, when he went into junior high in St. Paul, he was challenged, having missed sixth grade instruction in some of the basics. It was another difficult transition he faced and overcame.

As a young teenager, Bob's life had taken many turns in addition to being uprooted so many times. He was growing into his own persona and he enjoyed being involved in sports and church activities. He was finding his own happiness and was less intimidated in his home life. His parents were more focused on his young sister, which he admitted, "bothered him to a point," but they allowed Bob to join teams and activities, which, over time, gave him an increased sense of independence.

As one can imagine, friendships were also difficult to maintain with such a lifestyle. By the time he reached high school, his best friend named Bill in St. Paul, was always sad when Bob had to move away, but always welcomed him back when he returned. Bob's participation in high school sports was always readily accepted by the teams because he had some good abilities in the sports of track, football, and basketball.

Walking to school, Bob passed a house every day where a girl often came running down the steps and onto the sidewalk ahead or behind him. Lorraine Mae Heyn always seemed to be in a good mood, and he walked with her sometimes.

At the age of fifteen, Bob was doing well enough to miss a couple of his afternoon classes so he could report to his first job. He was hired by Swift & Company in St. Paul. It was a large meat processing center where he worked on an assembly line packaging various meat products. Bob rode a streetcar that passed four blocks from his school and went to downtown St. Paul. Then he got a transfer to South St. Paul. The trip took twenty-five minutes and cost seven cents. He repeated it in reverse on his way home in the dark. He worked eight-hour shifts and was paid less than $1 an hour, most of which he saved—while also paying $15 every month that was demanded by his father for room and board at home. By doing so, he seemed to earn some respect from his parents, while contributing to his own self-worth and sense of responsibility.

While he could hold a job at that age, he could not join the military. With so many American men and women joining the various branches of the service after the attack at Pearl Harbor, Bob Holmstrom longed to be one of them. But he would have to wait.

# 14

# Donovan's Web
# of Espionage

WORLDWIDE RECRUITING OF STAFF AND SECRET agents for the Office of Strategic Services was just the beginning of the web being woven by the irrepressible "Wild Bill Donovan." With the assistance of Canadian-born William Stephenson from the British Security Coordination, he had developed an agency that was divided into four branches:

1. Special Intelligence: Consisted of the secret agents who were assigned abroad to collect information on the countries of the Axis Powers and to determine the source of their economic support.

2. Special Ops: Assigned to conduct propaganda campaigns and to organize sabotage and guerilla warfare in occupied countries.

3. Foreign Nationalities: Based in New York, this group was tasked with searching ethnic groups living in the U.S. for political intelligence abroad and to recruit foot soldiers for covert ops.

4. Research and Analysis: The difficult and demanding job of making sense of the flood of information pouring into the OSS.[1]

In spite of his all-out efforts to organize the collection of intelligence for the United States, Donovan was faced with a good deal of resistance and hostility. He once stated, "I have greater enemies in Washington than Hitler."[2] He was "at odds," to put it mildly, with FBI Director J. Edgar Hoover from the start. Donovan's OSS was considered a "rogue agency" by Hoover and the military, and they felt it infringed upon their territory.

Bill Donovan had a penchant for rushing to get things done, often circumventing or otherwise ignoring protocol. This was highly disturbing to many, including Colonel Stuart Menzies, (code-named "C,") chief of the British Secret Intelligence Service (SIS,) as well as Churchill, and FDR at times. Yet "Wild Bill" would not be intimidated by anyone.[3] Donovan's web continued to grow.

The British Secret Service had shared a good degree of their experience and strategies with Bill Donovan. Their secret service, consisting of two divisions, served as both a road map and a textbook for intelligence espionage. The division code-named MI-5 generally dealt with domestic security, while MI-6 focused upon obtaining intelligence on foreign governments and armies, as well as activities of their adversary's agents.

When intelligence provides advance notice of an enemy's plans, size, or location, it can save many lives and often tip the scale in a conflict.

As Jennet Conant writes: "Bill Donovan trained his OSS agents to employ all aspects of intelligence, and they often used propaganda to achieve their goals. This could be accomplished by creating false reports in newspapers and dropping leaflets in hopes of convincing citizens to join the resistance or to discourage enemy troops. Similarly, radio signals could be jammed or static used to block a broadcast."[4]

She adds: "A variety of propaganda techniques has been used for centuries. Rumors or demoralizing reports have often succeeded in sabotaging the strength of an enemy's forces. Such sabotage is classified as 'Black Ops,' which was a basic tenet of Donovan's Office of Strategic Services. He employed and encouraged anything that could overcome an enemy."[5]

In 1942, Donovan took a giant step into the field of espionage. He hired a respected commercial chemist named Stanley Lovell to work in a lab where he was granted the freedom to create any sort of gadget or "spy aid" he could imagine. Lovell went to work and created all sorts of items including pistol silencers, miniature cameras disguised as pens, radios and recorders disguised as watches, invisible ink, and explosives disguised as a lump of coal (called a "Black Joe").[6]

Some of his creations were humorous, such as one he fashioned with the assistance of a "gland expert." It consisted of female sex hormones that could be injected into the food Hitler ate in order to make his mustache fall off and his voice to raise to soprano. (Clearly, that did not work or was never attempted.)

Other creations involving chemists included tasteless poisons that could be slipped into food or drinks, and knockout "K" pills. The U.S. DuPont Company produced the lethal "L" pill that would cause rapid death to a spy, agent, or any military personnel that had been captured by the enemy. Bill Donovan always carried one when traveling overseas.[7]

# 15

# Call to Duty

B OB HOLMSTROM HAD BEEN WORKING HIS WAY through high
school in St. Paul and on Minnesota's Iron Range as his
family moved back and forth. He was growing up through
the years of tumult around the world, and in 1941 the United States
had declared war on the Empire of Japan following their attack of
Pearl Harbor. There were long lines at the military recruiting offices
across the U.S. with men and women eager to serve their country.
Applicants welcomed the letter that began with "Greetings from the
President." Also, FDR ordered men between the ages of forty-five
to sixty-four to register for non-military service. Eventually, 16.1
million Americans would serve during World War II.[1]

Two warring forces had been formed as various countries lined
up on opposing sides: The Axis Powers, which included Germany,
Italy, and Japan, and the Allied Powers, which included Britain,
the United States, France, and the Soviet Union, as well as
Australia, Belgium, Bolivia, Brazil, Canada, China, Denmark,
Greece, Mexico, Netherlands, New Zealand, Norway, Poland,
South Africa, and Yugoslavia.[2]

At seventeen, Bob was in his senior year at Harding High School in St. Paul, and had done well in his studies despite the hardships of his family's frequent moves to and from northern Minnesota. His friendship with Lorraine had deepened and they often enjoyed both ice skating and roller skating together. When they walked to school, they held hands.

However, as their romance blossomed, there were other serious thoughts in the mind of Bob Holmstrom. He was anxious to serve his country. He explained, "What we did, we did voluntarily because we loved the United States. Kids today don't know because they didn't experience it. Things now are not the same. Everybody was working to help the war effort and everybody was talking about the war. My classmates were talking about joining up. We heard that the Navy had decent food and a bed to sleep in, but the Army guys had to sleep in a hole in the mud."

A good friend of Bob's shipped out as a cook on the USS *Ward*, a destroyer with a crew who were mostly Minnesota Reserves, not Navy personnel. As they patrolled the waters off the coast of Oahu, Hawaii, early on the morning of December 7, 1941, they spotted a Japanese Midget sub, which had no business being there. The *Ward* fired the first shots at an enemy combatant in the Pacific during World War II, and ultimately sank the sub.[3] (The gun that fired that first shot has been preserved and is on display on the west side of the Veteran's Service Building on West 12th Street in St. Paul, Minnesota.)

Two hours later, the Japanese attacked the U.S. Pacific fleet at Pearl Harbor. It was, as President Franklin Delano Roosevelt declared, "A date that will live in infamy."

"I had been reading about history and the war and how much they needed people to serve in the military," Bob explained. "I was seventeen years old and I decided to join the Air Corps. I took a streetcar to the Armory in St. Paul where I went through tests, [psychological and mechanical]. I was accepted, but I was still too young to enter the service, since you had to be eighteen. I had to wait another four months until my birthday on January 4. It seemed like the longest four months of my life."

Bob celebrated his eighteenth birthday on January 4, 1944. He had always loved airplanes and flying, so he was excited about the prospect of joining the military and hopefully flying a big plane. Finally, he could join the Army Air Corps (prior to it being called the Air Force,) and serve his country. At that time, the United States was engaged on several fronts—with the second World War raging in Europe, Africa and throughout the Pacific.

Bob graduated from Harding High School in St. Paul at the end of the term in January. He had never been out of the state of Minnesota, but he was about to embark upon a whirlwind journey to several locations in the United States for training before heading overseas. On February 4, his mother, father, and girlfriend Lorraine

Bob's senior high school photo

Bob's military induction photo

accompanied him to the bus in St. Paul. After goodbye's from his parents and a hug from Lorraine, he boarded the bus that would transport him to Fort Snelling, and as it pulled away, Bob admitted, "I felt kinda lonely right away."

Bob soon arrived at historic Fort Snelling, which stretches along a bluff on the shores of the Mississippi River across from St. Paul, Minnesota. Bob was no longer alone. Thousands were being inducted and long lines of recruits were funneled into various areas to be processed and cleared. Bob had "partially red hair" and the Air Corps cut it very short before he was sent to another long line of young men who were about to be bombarded with shots. While some of the others were alarmed by that process, Bob Holmstrom was cool, calm, and collected— confident that he had made the right choice.

There was yet another line—but this time Bob was really excited. He was about to get his uniform! After measurements were taken, he was issued a tan uniform, tan underwear, and shoes and boots as well. Everything fit! For a young man who had hardly ever gotten new clothes, this was a big deal, and he couldn't wipe the smile off his face. Although it had been a hectic day and Bob was tired, he felt really good about getting all those clothes. "They were in a bag so heavy, I could hardly carry it," Bob said. "We didn't have to wash them either—the Air Corps took care of that. Everything had your initials on it and the last four of your serial number. It made me feel good that I finally had this uniform and could get started on this war. I thought we could keep the war out of the United States, restore peace and quiet in Europe, and help people to get along."

Bob made friends with some of the guys during their six days at Fort Snelling, a few he thought he would never forget. But after they left and were sent to bases all over the U.S., he never saw any of them again.

Bob's new clothes

# 16

# Training 101

ON A BITTERLY COLD MORNING IN EARLY February, Bob
Holmstrom left Fort Snelling with many others on a bus
back to St. Paul, where they then boarded a train headed
for Texas. "It was a pretty good train ride. Several guys had
guitars and other musical instruments and they played real nice
music, which seemed to put everybody in a good mood," Bob
recalled. Along the way, their train occasionally had to pull over
onto a side track to allow supply trains to pass since they were
transporting military provisions. Sometimes Bob's train would
have to wait on the side track for several hours, and once
overnight before they could continue.

They stopped in Kansas City for a break and the recruits were
allowed to get off the train and stretch their legs a bit. It was an
eye-opening experience for Bob as he witnessed segregation in
full bloom there. When Bob attended school in Minnesota, he
knew of only one black family with children in school in St. Paul.
But in Kansas City, he saw several signs that read "No Blacks."
Black people were not allowed on buses or at restaurant counters
and they always had to give up their seats to whites if their

preferred seats were occupied. Bob said, "I couldn't understand why this was so. But there were no black people in our training courses and we had no black officers. The only blacks we saw on the base were cleaning the streets and latrines, or in the mess hall working as cooks and waiters."

Some of the guys had pooled their money and given it to one of them who volunteered to go get a bottle of whiskey for the rest of the trip. When it was time for the train to leave, a shrill whistle blew and the engine was running. As the wheels slowly started to turn, the guy had not returned with the whiskey. They were pulling away from the platform when around the corner of a building he came racing toward the train. He was out of breath, but tried to keep up with all the strength he had left. Several of the guys reached down and grabbed his arms, along with the bottle of whiskey, and they hauled him aboard. It was a close call—for him and their liquid refreshment.

They were now on the final leg of their journey and Bob was looking forward to getting to Texas. The novelty of a train ride had worn off after several days. As they got closer he thought, *It's going to be nice and warm!* They had passed Oklahoma City and crossed the border of Texas. The train pulled into the depot at Wichita Falls. Many buses were waiting. As the troops aboard gathered their gear and belongings, they were offloaded and each one was directed to a specific bus, which transported them to Sheppard Field Air Force Base. "Boy, was I in for a surprise!" remarked Bob.

They were escorted to their barracks, which were full of bunks and the bunks were assigned to specific persons. However, the first guy to reach his bunk got his choice of the upper or lower berth and Bob got the lower one. There was a foot locker for each guy at both ends of every bunk. Everything had to be folded and rolled up in it and your clothes hung properly. The big surprise for Bob came on the morning of his second day at Sheppard. Instead of the nice warm weather he had anticipated, he chuckled, "It was so cold in the morning that we had to wear long underwear!" By noon though, it was a different story and they peeled off the long johns as the temperature rose. But this was the norm in northern Texas at that time of year, and they all had to get accustomed to it.

Sheppard Air Force Base is the largest and most diversified training center in Air Education and Training Command. Its mission is to recruit, train, and educate quality people through military, technical, and flight training.[1] There, Bob Holmstrom and thousands of others were initially taught military basics. "We learned how to address officers, how to dress properly, how to make your bed properly (military style,) also how to polish your shoes and the brass on your belt buckle, and then how to set everything out for inspection," Bob said. "Keeping your bunk just so was expected."

He continued, "In the morning, we had to get up early to get in the shower, then get dressed quickly and line up on the company street outside the bunkhouse where we got our orders for the day [such as a long hike, classroom training, or report to the firing range]." The recruits at Sheppard were subject to physical training every morning to build up their strength. "We had to climb ropes and see how far we could jump and roll from a platform to see if you could stand the shock of the landing without hurting yourself," said Bob.

During the two and a half months of their training at Sheppard Field, unbeknownst to them, recruits were being scrutinized for those who might qualify as possessing "special skills and qualities" that would prove important during the war.

# 17

# In the Crosshairs

ONCE HIS BASIC TRAINING WAS COMPLETE at Sheppard Field, Bob was free to go on a two-week leave. He had met another guy from his home state who had an old car, so Bob and two others joined him on a road trip north. They all pooled their money to buy enough gas to get them to Minnesota. They had to use ration cards for gas at that time and more than once when they were short of cards, the station owner would look at those boys in uniform and give them a break.

Bob made his way by bus from the southern part of the state where the others left, and he headed to St. Paul. He had a pleasant reunion with his family and happy one with Lorraine. For the next several days, "She and I just bummed around and had a great time," Bob recalled with a smile. But, before he knew it, his leave was up and it was time to head south again.

It was April of 1944 and this time he was headed much farther south—to Laredo Air Force Base on the Rio Grande, across the river from Mexico. There was a plane at Laredo, the likes of which Bob had never seen. "It was really something," he remarked, "I had never seen anything that big!" It was the huge

B-24 Liberator. Plants in San Diego, Dallas, and the Ford Motor Company in Willow River, Michigan, were producing them at record rates. A number of little people were employed at the plants since they were able to climb inside the wings to install fuel lines, tanks, fire extinguishers, and wires for engines.[1]

Bob was sent to the Laredo AFB for gunnery school and advanced training, although he said, "I didn't know why and you didn't ask."

Although he had some experience hunting in northern Minnesota with a 22-caliber rifle, this was a whole new ball game. He was there to learn how to operate 50-caliber machine guns, but it began with a Browning shotgun that was mounted in a truck bed on either a turret or a fixed base. The recruits had to shoot at clay pigeons coming out at various angles from the woods. The plan was to train your eye to follow a moving target, react quickly, and help with your depth perception. "I got to be a good shot," Bob admitted.

Next, they went to classrooms, where they learned all of the parts of a 50-caliber machine gun, how to take it apart, and then reassemble it. After a good deal of practice, they had to do it blindfolded. Eventually, they had to do it blindfolded while wearing silk gloves, since while flying at 25,000-28,000 feet, you would lose the skin on your hands without protection from the cold. Silk prevented this from happening, and there was another reason for wearing silk gloves. If the machine gun malfunctioned, the gunner had to attempt to fix it. In order to accomplish that, he had to access a hole that was twelve inches long by six inches high, and the silk gloves provided an additional degree of dexterity. "In those circumstancess, it's gotta work right!" declared Bob.

They spent many hours of flight training, much of it in the dark, firing 850 rounds per minute. Before leaving Laredo, they were instructed and given experience with Thompson sub-machine guns and some Brownings as well.

The B-24 Liberator (Photo courtesy of Pima Air and Space Museum, Tucson, AZ)

# 18

# High Hopes

I N MAY OF 1944, BOB HOLMSTROM WAS ordered to report to another base approximately 150 miles to the northwest of Laredo. Eagle Pass Air Force Base, like Laredo, sat across the Rio Grande River from Mexico. As Bob traveled by bus between the two bases, he was excited about getting to Eagle Pass. For as long as he could remember, Bob Holmstrom dreamed of flying a plane. That is, to actually pilot one. Now his dream was about to come true as he was at Eagle Pass to learn how to do just that. He was about to learn how to be a fighter pilot.

He spent many weeks in the classroom, where he learned the specifics of things such as reading a compass and the ways in which weather and the stars relate to navigation. Also, he was introduced to the control panel and controls of the aircraft. After five months of training in the art of flying the AT-6 aircraft, Bob's hopes of piloting a plane were dashed.

President Franklin Roosevelt "abolished our class, just like that—said we had enough expendable pilots!" declared Bob, sadly. From that point on. Bob knew he would fly, but not as a pilot. Naturally disappointed, he nonetheless came to terms with

Bob in pilot training

it and took pride in the job he was assigned to do. From then on, he trained as a gunner.

The Eagle Pass Base was once an old cavalry base. When Bob was there, a number of large horses were also housed at the base since they were used by the nearby border patrol. Once in a while, Bob and some of his friends got to ride the horses, although Bob described them as "the meanest, orneriest horses I ever saw! They always wanted to return to the base." Bob recalled, "It was so hot there that a lot of guys passed out and had to be packed in ice to revive them. And we had to spend a lot of time outside in the sun with no hats, so we got badly sunburned on our heads and faces."

In December 1944, Bob was sent north to a base in Idaho.

# 19

# Flying Low

B OB HOLMSTROM WAS BEING TRANSPORTED TO the Air Force base at Mountain Home, Idaho, about fifty miles south of Boise. He described the train he was riding in as "pretty much like a cattle car. There were bunks lining the walls and a few small windows close to the ceiling. There were no seats and it was very uncomfortable."

Once he arrived at the base, which had been built four years previously, Bob was impressed with the buildings and the surrounding mountains. Soon after he was settled in the barracks, he was ordered to report to another building for a meeting. There he learned that he was being assigned to a bomber group, along with the nine other recruits in the room, who were to become his crewmates.

Bob described his crew as follows:

James Bingham, designated pilot. "He was a nice guy, married. Because he was a little older than most of the others, he was kind of a father figure to us. He inspired us to do better."

William Mitchell, copilot. "He was from Ohio, and like the pilot, a little older than the others. We looked up to both of them."

Richard Billings, navigator. "He was from Maine, and a heck of a guy. His knowledge of math was astounding. He did it all by pen and pencil, and he kept us safe."

James Malloy, bombadier. "He was quite a person. When we practiced a drop, he could put something within 100 feet of where it was supposed to go."

John Reinhold, radio operator. "He was from Council Bluffs, Iowa, and he was a mastermind with radios. There were so many of them aboard and he had to listen to several in order to intercept messages above twenty thousand feet."

Everett Mitchell, engineer/top turret gunner. "He was a character—quite a character—from Tennessee. His daddy was a moonshiner, so Everett knew how to make it—and he did. Whenever he could get some prunes or grapes or apricots, we got some good moonshine."

Richard Ecker, ball turret gunner. "He was from south St. Paul, Minnesota, so we were from the same neck of the woods. He had worked as a cattle buyer in the stockyards between Swift & Company and Armour & Company.

Paul Kovach from Pennsylvania and Charles McLain from North Carolina, waist gunners. "Kovach was more serious. McLain was happy-go-lucky. For a while, we only had one waist gunner while McClain served as the tail gunner."

Robert Holmstrom, nose gunner. "You have already met me."

"We were a great team and we all got along famously. Our pilot and navigator were the top ones in the whole group. We trained together as a crew right away."

As the assigned nose gunner, Bob had accepted that position with pride. He would be working in a turret which swiveled so he could see the pilot and engines, as well as having "the best view in the house." He had to attend a school in order to operate an Emerson electric turret with twin 50-caliber machine guns.

Many hours were spent on the shooting range as Bob learned to shoot at angles in the event that other planes would come from the front, side, or back.

There were some female pilots on the base, and their responsibilities entailed flying planes with a "sock" attached to the tail, which served as a target for the gunners in training. Bob explained, "Our guns were loaded with shells that had wax with a different color for each gun so you could tell who hit the target sock."

One day, all of the enlisted men were required to report for a dental exam, because as Bob explained, "At high altitudes, tooth decay could cause a heck of a toothache." He had to get four fillings.

On another day, recruits were subjected to a stamina test that involved going into a pressure chamber. Soon after entering, the pressure would change and each guy had to remove his oxygen mask, then count backwards from 100 to determine how many seconds he would last before passing out. Most wouldn't get very far (twelve to fifteen seconds) before getting disoriented. There was a dual reason for this test: in case something happened to your oxygen mask in flight, you had to have the wherewithal to locate an oxygen bottle in order to survive.

Bob and all of his crewmates passed. They learned that above ten thousand feet your oxygen mask would freeze to your face. "So when you removed it, you'd better be sure it was thawed out or your skin would come off with it and then you'd look like a chimpanzee!" Bob said.

With the classroom flight training and extensive gunnery practice Bob's crew had received while in Texas, they had sufficient knowledge to begin to put their skills to work in a real plane. They were thrilled when they proceeded to train in a B-24. The day of their first flight came and as they walked out to the plane, each one took a turn at spinning the prop on the #3 engine, which was done in order to get oil out of the lower cylinders so they would start easier. This was repeated next for the #4 engine, followed by the #2 and #1. This process started the generator and batteries so they had power for everything. Then they climbed aboard the huge aircraft and all but four took their assigned positions. Four of the positions were deemed unsafe for take-off and landing. They included the radio operator, bombardier, the tail gunner, and the nose gunner. As Bob was the nose gunner, he had to be one of the "party of four on the floor." They were instructed to sit in a tight row, as on a bobsled, so they were less likely to be tossed about.

As the engines started up, there was a great rumbling sound and the plane started to vibrate. Soon the B-24 started to roll and was it ever bumpy! The walls and floor were vibrating and it was quite uncomfortable, particularly for those on the floor. As the plane gained speed, the discomfort increased until at last—lift off! After the plane climbed to 500 feet, Bob and the other three scrambled to their positions. Bob worked his way forward to the nose and took his position behind the two 50-caliber machine guns. "I was so fascinated by what was happening all around us." he said. "The noise was deafening and in the nose the wind was too. But we were flying! We were really doing something good now! Really flying!"

After their first practice flight, they did many more until they were all comfortable with their duties. Bob and his crew were instructed to fly at low altitude over the mountains of Idaho, and they did many runs not far above the treetops. More than once, they flew as far away as the Gulf of Mexico, where they zoomed close to the surface of the blue water. Bob remarked, "I didn't know then why we had to fly so low—but I found out later."

# 20

# The Pot Boils Over

Worldwide tension continued to mount during the early 1940s as the Japanese Imperial Army, Hitler, Stalin, and Mussolini ramped up their brutal assaults on other nations and their people.

Following the Japanese attack on the U.S. Pacific Fleet in Pearl Harbor (Dec. 7, 1941,) both the U.S. and Britain, soon followed by China, declared war upon Japan. However, that did little to slow the Japanese army's progress on their expansionist policies as they forged ahead to bomb and/or otherwise invade several island nations.

In spite of combat with the U.S. and British forces, in April of 1942, the Japanese Imperial Army began the forced march of over 75,000 U.S. and Filipino troops to prison camps on the Island of Luzon in the Philippines. It was a journey of close to sixty-five miles in blistering heat. The prisoners were subjected to unspeakably ruthless abuse along the way to even worse conditions in a camp built for 10,000, as 60,000 were crammed into it. Ultimately resulting in the deaths of approximately 18,000 men, this horror became known as the infamous "Bataan Death March."[1]

Emboldened by their successes, the Japanese Imperial Army relentlessly continued their attacks on others. On October 7, 1943, they executed approximately 100 American POWs on Wake Island.[2]

In 1944, with the aid of the Allied Forces a few cracks began to appear in the Japanese Imperial Army defenses, when they had considered their army to be impervious. Persistent attacks and maneuvers by the U.S. and Allied Forces were finally having an effect on the size and capability of the Japanese army.

On the other side of the globe, Adolph Hitler was equally determined to expand his empire and to rid his homeland of the Jewish population. During the first years of the 1940s, he had invaded many European countries. In June of 1942, Hitler began the mass extermination of Jews by gassing them to death at Auschwitz and other concentration camps. By 1943, like the Japanese Imperial Army, the Nazi army was showing signs of war weariness and began to withdraw or surrender from cities they had occupied after many battles with the resistance and the Allied forces.[3]

Meanwhile, Benito Mussolini's visions of a reincarnated great Roman empire with himself as emperor were fading. Germany and its Axis allies had control of many of the lands he had hoped to occupy himself. It became apparent that he had neither the military strength nor the resources to compete, and when he did, he failed miserably. His exhausted troops and the population of his country lost faith in him.

By the end of 1933, Joseph Stalin had been successful in carrying out a reign of terror. He had forced between six and seven million peasant farmers and their families into starvation when they resisted having their land turned over to the state. Millions were exiled to Gulag camps and millions were simply executed. He had allied himself with Hitler but was double-crossed in June of 1941 when the Nazis surprised the Italian forces who were in no way prepared for such an attack. They suffered tremendous losses, and Stalin was devastated by Hitler's betrayal.[4]

The United States was drawn into the wars on both sides of the world after years of trying to remain neutral. It was becoming clear that Japan and Germany had both the capability and the desire to bring war to the shores of the American continent. A choice had to be made as to which theater of war to join first, Japanese or European. With Great Britain pleading for U.S. assistance, and with Hitler's merciless rampage across Europe, FDR opted to join the Allied Forces in Europe by initially providing military supplies to its Allies (Britain, France, and the USSR, among others.)

The first American troops arrived in North Africa on January 26, 1942.[5] From that point on, the United States was engaged in many battles in Europe while simultaneously becoming involved in the war in the Pacific. FDR had been building up the U.S. forces, supplies, equipment, ships, and aircraft. By March of 1942, the Japanese secret code was broken without their knowledge by U.S. Navy codebreakers. This provided an incredible advantage regarding the operations being planned by the Japanese Imperial Navy.

Five months after the Japanese attack on Pearl Harbor, U.S. forces were fighting the Japanese in the Battle of the Coral Sea, where both sides suffered losses, but the U.S. ended up strategically in a better position as a month later they decisively defeated the Imperial Japanese Navy in the Battle of Midway, between June 4-7, 1942. Many other battles continued to be fought in the Pacific, as the U.S. island-hopped, moving its bases ever closer to Japan.[6]

Young men from the United States being drafted into military service at that time would therefore be sent to the war in Europe or the one in the Pacific. They were generally not given a choice.

# 21

# O'er the Bounding Main

FROM MT. HOME, IDAHO, BOB HOLMSTROM and his crewmates
were sent by train to the Air Force base in Topeka, Kansas,
where they received final checkups, clothing, equipment,
and of course, more shots. A few days later, Bob and his crew were
escorted from the barracks back to the train station. This time they
were headed east—to Boston, Massachusetts. The largest ship in
the world at that time (besides the *Queen Mary*) called the *Ile de
France*, was docked in Boston Harbor, along with several other
vessels.

Bob thought, *Now I am going to leave the United States for
the first time.* His birthday and Christmas were coming up and
he admitted that he would miss the family and Lorraine. But he
was with his own crew now and that was comforting.

Bob and his crewmates were taken directly from the train to
the *Ile de France*, where they soon learned that they had some
prestige as members of the Army Air Corps, since they were
assigned to the "Sun Deck." The entire ship had been re-designed
to accommodate many thousands of troops, and the cabins were
lined with floor-to-ceiling bunks. Bob's crew had a room with

five double bunks and a salt water shower, while the guys on the lower decks had hammocks and a shower room down a long hall.

Most of the guys onboard had never been on a ship before, and being on one that huge was an overwhelming experience for them, but their excitement soon wore off. There was a good deal of hustle and bustle going on for the first few days. The wharves were full of trucks and equipment with men racing around as the ship was loaded with food, water, supplies for the ship itself, as well as military supplies. Then there were the ship's crew members as well as the thousands of troops, who all had to be checked in. Bob recalled, "I was excited about sailing on a ship of that size and being a part of such an enormous show of American military force." While most of the others were likely excited also, shortly after leaving the harbor, things changed.

They came face-to-face with the Atlantic Ocean and she greeted them with powerful winds and large swells, causing many onboard to succumb to sea sickness. "Not me," stated Bob, who was enjoying the ride. Meanwhile, it was another story on the lower decks for the guys in the hammocks. One can only imagine the mess if the guy on top vomited, which was a frequent occurrence. Bob added, "Some guys hardly got out of bed all the way across. It was seven to eight days. For those of us who could eat, the food was not good and many of us survived on Hershey bars and snacks. Those who were well enough were involved in physical training aboard the ship."

Along the eastern seaboard of the U.S., many other ships lined up to form a convoy. The *Ile de France* was in the middle of more than twenty ships spaced a half mile apart. There were no lights on the exterior of the ships and only very dim lights inside with window coverings. The U.S. ships did not have very good radar equipment then and the radios were full of static. There was very little communication between the ships because of nearby subs with

Germans who were anxious to intercept messages. "We were forced
to use flashing lights and Morse code or flags for communication
in the daytime when we determined there were no subs in the
vicinity. At night, it was imperative that all lights were out and it
was forbidden to light a cigarette outside. It was total darkness,"
Bob said.

The vast majority of the troops had never been on salt water
before, and as they sailed across the depths, the sea got rougher.
"It was one storm after another. Dark clouds filled the sky so
there was little daylight. The waves were sometimes as high as
the Sun Deck," recalled Bob. "On the decks below it had to be
terrifying. The north Atlantic had a salt smell—and there was a
cold mist always. Because of the high wind and waves, I never
got to the back of the ship."

Those who were not seasick would get together and play cards
or shoot dice, and Bob was introduced to gambling, although as
an observer not a participant. He also never smoked like so many
others did, and he and members of his crew, having some rank
over most of the others, were assigned guard duty to patrol the
decks at night and make sure no one lit up a cigarette after dark,
which could be detected many miles away. Bob stated, "We were
like little MPs."

# 22

# Land Ho!

A FTER A WEEK OF SAILING ACROSS AN inhospitable Atlantic, the *Ile de France* arrived at the "Firth of Clyde," which is located along the coast of Scotland with the largest and deepest coastal waters in the British Isles. This made it vital to Navy operations.[1] Bob described it as "a beautiful sight, not only because it was great to see land again, but because of the beautiful colors of the grass and the rugged coastline."

However, danger was lurking below! As the big ship entered the bay, a German sub boldly followed it in. It was an extremely dangerous stand-off for several hours. No one was allowed to debark the ship and emergency precautions were in force. Bob said, "Ultimately, the sub was sunk. We heard it was done by the British."

After a couple of days, the troops were transferred from the ship and boarded onto a train headed for Glasgow, Scotland. Bob recalled the trip, saying, "That train was a marvelous experience. There was a private room for sitting with two benches in each one, so our crew was split up, but everyone was comfortable. It was a real nice train for that time. How the military ever kept track of all of us was an amazing thing, really."

After a short time in Glasgow, the troops re-boarded and they headed toward an Air Force Base located in Cheddington, England. Bob said, "We were excited about seeing the country. Scotland was so nice. The houses were pretty and the colors were beautiful. There was no sign of war. When we arrived at the base, we were welcomed by a U.S. Army band playing on the platform!"

Once they had been established in their assigned quarters, they were allowed to walk around the base, and they spotted a large number of B-24 bombers parked on the surrounding fields. The B-24s were newer than the B-17s which had previously been used extensively in the war.

Bob was impressed with the base at Cheddington. "It was kind of a comfortable place to be," he said. "We lived in Quonset huts, eighty people in each, with double bunks, foot lockers at the end of each, and a shower building a half block away. There were no doors in the shower room and in the morning it was quite cold [30 degrees F] so you got out of there in a hurry. The toilets were just open troughs with water running through them and no seats or partitions. You had to position yourself on a wall above the trough. If you had to go to the latrine after dark, since there were no lights, you had to use a flashlight which was bent downward at the end with a pinhole for the light, that was red so it was not detectable by radar."

There were underground bomb shelters on the base and, as Bob recalled, "Sometimes you would just get to bed and then hear the siren and have to race out to the shelter because the Germans were flying over. It was always close. Because it was well-camouflaged, they never hit the base. The first time I heard an air raid signal—it was really loud; I never heard anything like it! There would be a complete blackout, and we would have to use a few of those L-shaped flashlights to find our way to the shelter."

Bob and his crew had to make many practice flights at

Cheddington, so that their navigator could familiarize himself with the weather conditions and the stars. They had British counterparts who flew twin-engine planes called "Mosquitos," made of plywood with Rolls Royce engines, and Canadians who flew rugged single-engine planes called Haviland DHC2 Beavers.

Bob remembered an incident that occurred during one of their training flights; "We were on oxygen at 13,000 feet and I happened to look out the window just as a British Mosquito flew fifty feet from us and did a slow roll—just showing off! Then he disappeared!"

****

Bob's crew had one of the first FM radios. Two U.S. inventors named Stephen H. Simpson and DeWitt R. Goddard dubbed the radio with the name "Joan Eleanor," ("Joan" being the first name of Simpson's girlfriend; "Eleanor" being the first name of Goddard's wife). "Joan" was a hand-held radio transmitter that was used on the ground, while "Eleanor" was the receiver used in the air while in flight. It was similar to a walkie-talkie, but it had a high frequency radio signal used behind enemy lines. Joan's signal could not be detected by the enemy since its signal went straight up. Eleanor also could not be detected and it transmitted to 40,000 feet with a sixty-mile radius. It proved an invaluable tool and was top secret. The U.S. shared it with the British, who used it extensively for communicating with the French and Belgian underground.

On Bob's plane, there were five different radios. During assembly and take-off, there were no radio communications at all. Once in the air at high altitude, the radio operator could sometimes locate a U.S. signal. He could broadcast it over the intercom, and despite a lot of static, Bob said, "We got to hear some good American music, which always brought a big smile to our faces."

## 23

# The First Five

**A**FTER MANY TRAINING FLIGHTS FOR BOB and his crew, the time came for their first mission. "We never knew exactly what cargo was on board," stated Bob, "but our first mission was almost like training and we did know we were dropping leaflets over occupied areas. It was American propaganda to counteract the propaganda that the Germans were spreading."

"Our first mission lasted about six hours, and it went well," Bob remembered. "We flew at a higher altitude—20,000 feet, dropping leaflets over the villages and towns of France and Belgium. From where I was in the nose, I could look back at the pilot and I could see all four engines. The view was spectacular as we flew through the mountains. Having two 50-caliber machine guns with a console that controlled the turret was a unique device at that time. It was like a video game nowadays."

Take-off was about 9:30 pm. After the routine check of equipment, everyone knew what he had to do, and they were excited about it. There was 100% radio silence and no lights. Bob recounted the following:

*The engines revved up and the plane turned onto the runway. After one quick flash from the control tower, the plane was bouncing as we accelerated and rolled toward the trees at the end of the runway. We should be up by now! Feeling kinda afraid and excited, you wondered if you were gonna make it. At the very last minute, the pilot pulled up the wheels and we were in the air! We took a few branches off the trees.*

*Our first mission was not particularly far or dangerous, and we were told that we usually would not be privileged to know the exact location we were flying to, but this time we heard it was northern France. Once we got over the English Channel, we had to test-fire our guns. When we reached our target location, the moon was high in the sky, bright as a floodlight.*

*At five miles up, we dropped eight to ten large cylinders containing leaflets out of the bomb bay. Instantly lighter, and the plane popped up in the air. At two thousand feet, barometric pressure would explode the containers.*

The leaflets would scatter in the air like big snowflakes as they fluttered to the ground below in small towns and villages. The purpose of the leaflets was to inform people and encourage them to join the resistance, and there were also surrender documents and newsletters for patriots.

"I can tell you," said Bob, "it was an exhilarating sensation to be up there and do that at the age of nineteen! Doing what you're supposed to do—looking and observing. I was an official 'sight-seer' and I felt pretty important. There was danger to it, though. The British dropped incendiaries and sometimes you could see a town burning seventy-five to a hundred miles away. It was important to remember the time, direction, and how far away you thought it was from where we were."

He added, "In the meantime, the navigator would come

through every six-to-eight minutes and tell you about the area below and how many kilometers it would be to an orphanage, monastery, or other place of refuge and the direction to go to find that place in case you had to parachute out."

Following each of their missions, the crew was ordered to report to a room for de-briefing, which involved telling their superiors what they had observed. Details were important, and to that point, the men were offered "liquid encouragement" in the form of whiskey (cognac) to relax them (and their tongues.) Even the smallest recollection could be significant, and it may have been something a guy had noticed subliminally that only came to mind when he or someone else recalled something. Bob detested the cognac, and vowed that after he got out of the service, he would never drink it again.

As their missions went on, they were further and further away and not always without a hitch. They took anti-aircraft fire and holes would appear in several places on the plane as shrapnel tore through it. Bob remarked, "We got through pretty good though, and always got back safe."

As dangerous as direct fire and anti-aircraft fire was, often equally dangerous were take-offs and landings. On the way out, the plane was overloaded with supplies, while on the way back, it was low on fuel. To add to the danger, it was usually foggy both ways.

When they were not flying missions, there were more training flights and classroom sessions on things like survival, and customs and languages of countries they would likely fly over. In the case of an airman being hit by small pieces of shrapnel, which was a frequent occurrence, providing it was not in a critical location, one could remove it rather easily with a tool called a "curette," which was part of the first aid kits. It is a hand tool approximately five-to-six inches long with a small scoop on the tip which is used to scrape tissue in order to remove small foreign objects.[1] It worked fine on tiny pieces of shrapnel, and many guys would use it if hit in the arm or leg, then quickly throw some sulfa powder and a bandage on and continue their duties.

There was morphine for anything especially painful, and each kit also contained that "L" (lethal) pill in case they got shot down or had to bail out over enemy territory. Bob said, "Some claimed it might have been better if they hadn't tried to deal with their injuries themselves and just waited until they were back on base. If they had gone to the infirmary, they may have qualified for extra benefits later for being wounded during service."

Bob's crew was sent to other areas for their next four missions. They were never told what the cargo consisted of or what their target area was, but they continued to do their jobs and deliver the cargo to the people on the ground. The first mission had clearly been to an area designated as "low risk," since they had taken no fire along the way. However, that changed on successive missions, where flak, anti-aircraft fire, and machine gunfire from enemy planes was common.

# 24

# Free Time Escapades

NOW AND THEN BOB AND HIS CREW, as well as some members of the ground crew, were allowed to go into town. The guys on the ground were unsung heroes, repairing and patching up most every plane that made it back to base so it would be ready to fly again, usually on the following day. "There was never a bad word among us. We were like brothers—only better. Your life depended on them," Bob said.

Before they were allowed to go to town, they were lectured about British customs and expectations of their behavior. The first time Bob left the base with a buddy to go to a pub, they each got a pint of warm beer, since it was all that was being served. As Bob remembered, "We saw a couple of guys playing darts and they asked us if we wanted to join them. They seemed like nice fellows, so we agreed. They explained the rules, that included shooting a 'double one' (difficult to do) in order to start playing. The losers had to buy a round of beer. That should have been a clue to us) I bought the first round. My buddy bought the next."

The pubs closed at 10:00 p.m. and they had to be back on base by 11:00 p.m.. A couple of times they were permitted to stay overnight at the "Boar's Head," which had a B&B upstairs with feather beds in the rooms and a bathroom in the hallway. The pub served warm beer and prior to closing time, they would offer a last drink of spirits called "NEAT," which was a straight shot. Bob said, "Most people thought it was a treat. Not me."

Sometimes they would get three or four days off and were able to take a train to London. "It didn't cost much and you got a nice compartment," Bob recalled. He got to see several landmarks in the city and beautiful countryside along the way.

"I met a lot of nice British people," he said. "I was able to go to the church by the base where a kind couple invited a friend and me to their home more than once."

Bicycles were a primary mode of transportation for the local people around the base, but during the war, no more were being produced, so they were few and far between. Bob had saved some money and he was fortunate in being able to purchase one from a local man. He said, "You had to get a permit to have one. There were many canals with four-foot sidewalks on both sides in that part of the country and small barges would move things back and forth. The sidewalks were a nice place to ride a bike."

One night, after he received a permit, Bob rode his bicycle along with a friend who also had one, to a pub where they enjoyed "many pints of warm beer." On the way back, Bob swerved, and into the canal he went. It was totally dark and try as he might, he couldn't locate the bicycle. He had to hitch a ride with his buddy on his bike. It was cold, amplified because Bob was sopping wet.

Things got worse the next morning. His uniform had shrunk! With "his tail between his legs," he had to walk to a supply building in that short, wet uniform. Once there, he had to explain what had happened and request another.

There were no extra U.S. uniforms on hand, so he was issued a British military jacket.

**IMPORTANT—READ AND UNDERSTAND**

1. **Never** ride your bicycle after darkness without a tail light and fixed head light.
2. **Never** ride two persons on your bicycle.
3. **Never** ride your bicycle without this permit on your person.
4. **Never** change the registration number or repaint this bicycle in any way.
5. **Never** leave your bicycle unlocked because you will be held pecuniarly responsible.

**BE CAREFUL**

BICYCLE PERMIT. 363

Name  Robert E Holmstrom

Rank and Serial Number  Sgt

Bicycle Number  48288

License Number  C 50

Date Issued  7 March 1945

WILLIAM M LILE, 1st Lt OMPr.

Bicycle instructions and permit

Because bicycles were scarce and valuable, Bob had to return to the canal the next day to search again, and he found it. He fished it out, knowing that he could easily re-sell it, and he soon did.

While he had to wear the British military jacket, Bob got called "Limey" by others.

# 25

# Spies, Supplies, and Not Just Another B-24

S OON AFTER THE OFFICE OF STRATEGIC SERVICES (OSS) had gotten the go-ahead on October 19, 1943 to deliver supplies, equipment, and spies to the resistance, Bill Donovan forged full-speed ahead, hiring more agents and spies to add to the many thousands he had already placed around the world. He would need large numbers of courageous men and women who were willing to risk their lives for the people of enemy-occupied European countries.

Working in cooperation with the British Special Operations Executive (SOE), massive preparations had to be made while they planned a course of action. Both organizations were headquartered six stories underground in London with the SOE taking charge of obtaining the myriad supplies and equipment being requested by covert groups on the ground.

The OSS was tasked with obtaining agents and spies to train and work with those of the resistance. There was propaganda to be produced in leaflets (called "nickels") and over radio stations, plus a large number of false passports, counterfeit money, food ration cards, etc. Aiding the resistance with guerilla warfare was also part of their duty when necessary. These missions were code-named "Operation Carpetbagger."

The Special Operations Executive in London was in charge of establishing a command center for goods, equipment, and supplies. A large warehouse located in the countryside was being stocked with weapons, bicycles, clothing, food, radios, blankets, shoes, documents—anything that would be requested by the people of the resistance. Their needs were called in by a secret radio system and they were notified in the same way as to the time and location of the air-drop. The items were collected and prepared for distribution by a multitude of people working in the warehouse to pack them into large thickly-corrugated cardboard cylinders, boxed packages, and well-insulated baskets. They would have to withstand the impact of a 300- to 400-foot drop from a low-flying B-24.

It was determined that they were going to need large planes with a long range that had the ability to fly at low altitudes, and the Consolidated B-24 Liberator heavy bomber was designated to fit the bill. However, modifications would have to be made to the plane's original design, since the Carpetbagger planes were destined for extremely dangerous top-secret special operations.

As a result, the ball turret was removed from these special-ordered planes, and it was replaced with a smooth metal shroud called a "Joe Hole," which was forty-four inches in diameter and forty-eight inches at the end. During flight, the hole was covered by a hinged plywood door. When the plane reached the drop-off site, a green light would flash and the agent would slide down the "Joe Hole" and parachute into the darkness.[1]

A couple of other modifications were also made to the "Carpetbagger aircraft" (often referred to as "ships"). The bomb bay

Top: B-24 with open bomb bay (Photo courtesy of Pima Air and Space Museum, Tucson, AZ)

Bottom: Carpetbagger B-24 (Photo courtesy of Charles Pinck, 2018 President of OSS)

area was cleared for the storage of the containers and packages while in flight. Windows were fitted with black-out curtains wherever possible. Then the exterior of those planes were painted entirely black, which had been determined to evade radar detection and that of troops on the ground or by enemy aircraft in the darkness.

They were ready for covert missions in the night.

## 26

# New Faces in Old Places

W HILE AT CHEDDINGTON, THERE WERE A FEW changes in Bob's crew. He recalled, "We were somehow flying at the wrong altitude on one of our missions, which was very dangerous because the British would accidentally shoot you down. Our tail gunner was a drinker and kind of a renegade. He slid open the door on the turret and shot a flare gun to alert the British, but the flare burned a hole on the tail. It was the radio operator's job to alert the Brits, not his. He was re-assigned to another detail."

When they had completed their first five missions, Bob and his crewmates were eligible for their first Air Medal. While it would have been presented to them almost immediately, a dangerous situation was developing. Intel had informed those in command at Cheddington that the Germans were getting too close for comfort and may soon discover the base.

Medals would have to wait. It was time to move.

When they got all of the planes and equipment together, a large force moved to the Harrington base. Upon landing, one of the other planes crashed, killing all on board except one. His name was Marsema Butts, and he was transported to the infirmary. Meanwhile, the copilot of Bob's crew was "kind of a nervous guy," and he quit. "He just couldn't take it anymore and was reassigned," said Bob. When Marsema Butts was treated and released from the infirmary, he was assigned to replace the copilot who had quit in Bob's crew. "Butts was a good guy, and we welcomed him. He became part of our family."

There was still an opening in the crew—the tail gunner position, since the former one had been relieved of that duty. While the nose gunner had "the best view in the house," the fascination had worn off for Bob Holmstrom. "I was kind of anxious to get in another part of the ship instead of seeing all that flak coming at us," he said. "I could stand watching it from the back because then we were past it."

Bob had to go to "another school on the base to learn how to operate the tail turret." He added, "It was twelve to thirteen hours a day. There was no shortage of education. The tail was 100 feet from the nose of the ship, and the turret was completely different from that of the nose. It was hydraulic and faster than the one in the nose. It went quickly up, down, and sideways. When it was backwards, your back was exposed, but I liked it there."

# 27

# Ready, Willing, and Able

BILL DONOVAN'S SECRET MISSIONS BECAME a reality with the creation of "Operation Carpetbagger." It originated as an attachment to the 492nd bomb group at Harrington Air Force Base which was in a well-hidden, highly secret location in England.

Bob Holmstrom's bombardment group (the 406th) had been ordered to report to Harrington in January of 1945. Once there, Bob and his crew were in for a surprise. Their quarters were tents—a big step down from their comfortable lodgings in the Cheddington Quonset huts!

Lieutenant Colonel (Lt. Col.) Robert Fish was the commander of the 801st Bombardment Group at Harrington, and several carefully-selected squadrons of airmen, including Bob's crew, were told to report to Headquarters, where Lt. Col. Fish was to address them. Wondering what was up, there was a degree of tension in the air. As soon as Lt. Col. Fish entered the room, you could hear a pin drop.

He got straight to the point by basically describing the special operations. Details were withheld, except that he stressed the

Bob in front of his "home tent"

desperate need for delivering supplies to the Resistance and for propaganda to convince others to join the movement. He did, however, state the dangers involved in flying these missions, which could only be performed on moonlit nights, with no lights, at low altitude over enemy territory. Then he asked for volunteers (with the understanding that there would be no repercussions for those who declined, just re-assignment.)

Bob Holmstrom and his crewmates all eagerly volunteered.

When those who declined to volunteer had left the room, Lt. Col. Fish addressed the remaining group, announcing, "Gentlemen, you will be taking part in highly-classified covert operations." A brief silence ensued as they tried to process what they had just heard. He then told them that they would be part of the OSS, flying secret missions code-named "Operation Carpetbagger."

Aerial view of Harrington AFB tent city

Lieutenant Colonel Fish continued to stress that "secrecy was of the utmost importance." Therefore, as Bob stated, "We were highly encouraged to keep our mouths shut." Next, Lt. Col. Fish informed them that they would be "flying dangerous top-secret missions," and that if asked, they should respond that they are "plotting courses—and leave it at that." There were questions, but few answers as he told them that they had been chosen because each of them possessed the exceptional traits and skills necessary to carry out these missions. Finally, he reiterated the need for absolute secrecy, and that a court martial, or worse could result for anyone who may jeopardize these important missions that hopefully would help to win the war. Then he wished them good luck.

When Lt. Col. Fish exited the room, the pilot of Bob Holmstrom's crew confirmed that it was an honor to be chosen to serve in this manner. They were all surprised and mystified by this unexpected revelation, while at the same time feeling a sense of pride that they had been judged worthy of carrying out clandestine operations.

When asked if he had any fear of death at that point, given the nature of their assignment to such a dangerous operation, Bob immediately responded, "Oh no! We were just going to win the war. We were going to do it, then go back home!" No doubt many other young men felt the same, but they did not all return home.

Between flying test missions and preparing for their upcoming assignments, Bob and his crew were schooled in some basics of the languages and customs of the countries they would be flying over...in case they went down.

Over the next several days, they had to fly several practice runs at night so the navigator could get his bearings with the stars. They did not fly in formation. They took off alone, into the darkness, with no escort, and they returned alone—that is, if they returned.

Nonetheless, Bob Holmstrom and his crew were ready, willing, and able.

# 28

# A Royal Tribute

URING WORLD WAR II, AIRMEN WERE GRANTED the Air Medal for every five missions they flew in combat. Bob Holmstrom and his crew had completed their first five missions while at the Cheddington base, but the awarding of their medals had to be postponed due to their unexpected orders to move to the Harrington base.

Germany had invaded the Netherlands on May 10, 1940, and the reigning queen, Wilhelmina, along with her family and cabinet members, fled to England for sanctuary.[1] She was there when the 492nd bomb group arrived at Harrington. Since the presentation of their medals for their first five missions had been delayed, an invitation was extended to Queen Wilhelmina to visit the air base and perform the presentation honors. She graciously accepted.

So it was that Queen Wilhelmina herself pinned the medals on the uniforms of Bob Holmstrom and each of his crewmates, commending them for their first five missions. That certainly made it special and they were all understandably proud.

Then they looked forward to the next five missions.

Air Medal presented to Bob and his crew

# 29

# Behind the Scenes

LTHOUGH BOB HOLMSTROM AND THE REST of his crew were used to flying in a B-24, the one they were assigned to fly for the Carpetbaggers was distinctive due to the modifications that had been made to the interior in order to accommodate vast quantities of supplies. They all took pride in their plane and the missions they hoped to accomplish.

The crew of Bob Holmstrom's B-24J had completed fifteen daytime dry runs. In addition, they had accomplished five nighttime cross-country runs, each with a duration of no less than two and a half hours, the fourth of which was made entirely by pilotage, which required them to fly without the use of radio and radar equipment. Each crew member was put to exact standards throughout their training in every facet of his performance, followed by an oral exam given by an officer, directed primarily toward the pilot and the navigator.

Meanwhile, much had been accomplished by the OSS Air Ops Headquarters in London. There was a large map on the wall, pinpointing locations of targets and other significant things such as mountains, rivers, lakes, railroads, bridges, factories, military bases and warehouses, etc. It was Bill Donovan, as head of the OSS, who dealt with the numerous requests for a variety of supplies and equipment. These requests were from OSS agents in the field who were working undercover with the resistance. Donovan and his staff screened the requests and focused on those that appeared most urgent. Then they would be filtered again, taking into account location, weather conditions in the area, and proximity of the intruding enemy. A senior staff member ultimately determined the targets.

On the morning of a Carpetbagger mission, the SOE warehouse, located in the countryside, was a beehive of activity. Numerous well-insulated boxes, cylinders, and baskets were being carefully packed as the items inside them were checked off a list. It was a well-coordinated event with a great many OSS staff members working in sync toward a deadline for loading them all into trucks. They were then transported to the Harrington base.

# 30

# The Big Day

ON THE MORNING OF THEIR FIRST Carpetbagger mission Bob Holmstrom and his crewmates were allowed to sleep a little longer since they were going to be up all night, but everyone awoke early. This was the day they had worked so hard for and looked forward to for a very long time. Now they would be dropping not just leaflets, but boxes, baskets, and cylinders full of supplies to the people of the resistance. This was the critically important work for which the Carpetbaggers had been specially trained.

Throughout the afternoon, their navigator was busy plotting targets, and checking for any known flak in the drop-zone area. The rest of the crew was required to perform a thirty-minute test flight of the aircraft to make sure the plane was ready to go. Upon their return, the trucks, loaded with supplies to drop, were directed onto the field to begin loading all of the packages and cylinders (many weighing fifty-to-one-hundred pounds each,) into the bomb bay of the big black B-24J. Leaflets were delivered in bundles of four thousand, and there would be six-to-ten bundles of them (depending on stock at hand, length of flight, and anticipated time over enemy territory.) Each of the containers and packages had to be fitted with a harness, then a parachute was attached.

Bob and his crew were allowed some free time in their tent quarters during the late afternoon. That was when most of them wrote letters home. However, no details were to be given, and all letters had to be censored by their pilot. While they could have taken a brief nap, they were too excited to sleep for even a short while. Their many months of training were about to pay off with a secret mission that could help many people and most likely save lives.

It was time to "gear up."

## 31

# Dressed for Success

PERSONAL PREPARATIONS FOR FLIGHT INVOLVED a wardrobe of clothing items. "It took so long to get dressed!" Bob said. "There were many layers due to the high altitudes where we had to fly before we headed down to a very low level so we could deliver our load." That meant long underwear, socks, a woolen shirt, trousers, felt shoe inserts, a jacket, scarf, gloves, rayon glove inserts, mittens, a helmet, goggles, oxygen mask, a Mae West inflatable life vest, chest-pack parachute, and chute harness. Those were just the standard items.

There were also "heated items" for high-altitude flying. These included: a heated jacket insert, heated trouser insert, heated shoe inserts, and heated gloves. Of course, each item had to be put on in a certain order and connected to a lead cord that was plugged into the plane's electrical system. While that may seem a luxury, it was actually a necessity. With no other heat system inside the plane, at high altitudes, everyone on board would have frozen to death.

The heated items were generally worn regardless of the planned flight altitude, since you never knew when you may have to climb to a higher altitude to evade weather conditions, anti-

Bob (*rear, 2nd from left*) and five crewmates, "geared up" and ready to fly

aircraft fire, or enemy planes. They sometimes wore a "flak helmet," which was designed to protect the ears and head from injury, since many American bomber crews suffered serious injury or death from shrapnel wounds. These special helmets had metal, felt-lined ear flaps to protect the earphones that had to be worn for communication.

There was a special detail of people called "dressers" assigned to assisting crews in getting outfitted for a flight. "Sometimes it was a regular tug-of-war to get everything on!" Bob explained. "We had so many clothes on, and it all had to be just right to get your hands around and do your job."

Finally, at that point, Bob and his crew were ready to go. They were well-trained and well-dressed.

# 32

# Secret Knights in the Night

AFTER BOB AND HIS CREW WERE DRESSED, they went back to Headquarters for a final briefing, during which an officer, along with Lt. Col. Fish, provided some reminders, along with their confidence in the crew, and their high hopes for a successful mission. Then they synchronized their watches.

The sun had set and evening was being felt by a definite chill before the sky faded to dark bluish-black just ahead of the ground fog which was creeping onto the field. That was when Bob and his crew were escorted to their waiting aircraft, which they had named "The Night Knight." Their clothing and gear was cumbersome, but they all took their turn at spinning the props in a planned sequence in order to assist the four engines in starting up. Then they climbed aboard and took their places, having to squeeze between the many cylinders, baskets, and packages that had been methodically crammed into the bomb bay.

"While we had many previous training flights and test flights, this was different," Bob said. "This one was real—our first real mission! We were rarin' to go!"

Bob posing "dressed " next to his plane,
the "Night Knight"

After getting the green light from the control tower, all four engines rumbled loudly and emotions ran high as they taxied out on the runway. "There was naturally some concern," Bob recalled, "but not fear. We were so well-trained and judged to be among the best. We were confident in our abilities and those of our crewmates to get the job done!"

The sound of the tires spinning ever faster intensified while the walls of the aircraft shuddered in its burden with the heavy load it was carrying. They all noticed a difference in the way the plane handled and performed as it lumbered down the runway and seriously labored to remove itself from the ground.

Everyone became concerned about their chances of a successful take-off. And there it was—the end of the runway—just as the wheels left the surface! Barely missing the trees again, there was a collective sigh of relief because the danger was real and the young men aboard knew that once again, they were in luck. They were then able to start their climb upward, and when they reached 500 feet, the four crewmen moved from the floor to their posts, with Bob as the tail gunner. Their plane climbed through the dark of night to a cruising altitude of 20,000 feet.

Only the pilot and the navigator knew the exact location of their drop, but it would be a few hours before they arrived. It had taken a good amount of training in the dark to acclimate themselves to the interior of the modified plane. Along with the instruments and guns the crew needed to operate, they had to condition their eyes to become more keenly aware of geographic landmarks in addition to enemy planes.

They had all been schooled in the various aircraft they may likely encounter and the necessity of properly identifying them and their location when first sighted in the air. They were trained to identify another plane by its type ("Messerschmitt" or "Mosquito," for example) followed by its location as with the hands of a clock (such as "three o'clock high"). Everyone needed to be on the lookout at all times.

Anti-aircraft fire was an ever-present danger for any plane flying over enemy-occupied territory. Huge JU88 canons spewed out explosive shells high into the sky. From a plane, they appeared as black puffs of smoke called "flak." However, they were much more than just black puffs—they were full of deadly and destructive shrapnel. A direct hit would usually result in a fiery explosion of the plane. Often there were black puffs

Crew with oxygen masks

everywhere and it was a testament to the skill of any pilot who could safely snake his aircraft through a field of devastating flak. It was a common occurrence for pieces of metal, large and small, to rip through the aircraft from any direction or for bullets from enemy aircraft or guns on the ground to bore through the plane until they hit something or someone. Otherwise, they whizzed right through and exited on the opposite side.

The use of the Norden bombsight was invaluable since it allowed the navigator to pinpoint the target almost exactly, although as they got closer to their target, the danger increased exponentially. The enemy was forever on the offense, trying to prevent missions such as this one.

## 33

# Sounds of the Forest

F AR BELOW THE GIANT BLACK BIRD THAT WAS winging its way toward the drop zone, the ground was frozen. No snow had fallen because perhaps it was too cold to do so. But there was frost everywhere in the forest. Every branch and twig donned a thick layer, and there was a sparkling blanket of it on the ground. The winter of 1944-45 in that part of the world was the coldest in one hundred years. Yet there was life in the forest. Animals who had learned to adapt to the bitter cold were there. Then there were others who struggled to merely cope with it. These were the people who were fighting in resistance to the occupation of their country, and they were working in coordination with the Carpetbaggers. Their pleas for assistance had been heard and approved through radio communication with the SOE and the OSS. Help was on the way.

A couple of hours earlier, there had been some subtle noise as cars, trucks, and wagons had been moved into place. This was done with a minimum of sound, and it was a well-rehearsed ritual. The price of sound was dear, and many would pay the price if even one violated the silence. They waited, some in the vehicles, some amongst the trees, all bitterly cold and miserable in their hunger and exhaustion, yet so desperate for the supplies that were to come that they risked their lives and often those of their family members to be there.

Once they were in position, the only sounds for a very long time were the natural sounds of the forest of which they had become a part. An owl calling out would break the palpable silence of the night, as would a squirrel or other small animal as it crept along the forest floor. The occasional sharp snap of a twig broken at the hoof of a deer, or something larger would garner an uneasy tension among the people in wait. Then at last—the distant hum of engines alerted them to prepare for an imminent drop of everything they had waited for, and sometimes even people to assist them in their efforts.

As the plane approached, the roar of the engines was a symphony to their ears. It was their salvation, and many could not have survived without the supplies being delivered to them in that designated clearing. With only the moonlight and the few flashlights held by people positioned on the ground to guide it, the huge black plane passed just overhead, as they expected, then in the distance, it turned.

The Carpetbaggers had been flying for several hours and the moon in its full beauty was high in the sky. Bright as a spotlight, it aided the crew onboard Bob's plane as they neared their target area. They had been descending for some time and flying with no lights. The plane was going lower and lower, down to 400 or 300 feet while it slowed to 120-130 miles per hour—nearly stall speed. Bob commented, "It was a treacherous time for getting shot at. We were very close to the target—at great risk to us."

But then they spotted lights on the ground in a pattern they recognized. They had just flown over the target area, then did a slow turn and circled back.

The big plane was heading directly back over the drop zone, and soon the doors opened on the belly of the plane and its cargo was released. The treasured items fell from the sky like gifts attached to umbrellas as the parachutes opened. The drop was quick and right on target. As soon as most of the items hit the ground, the people gathered with practiced efficiency to load everything into the waiting vehicles and wagons.

With the rumble of the plane growing dim in the distance, the only sounds in the forest were those of the vehicles pulling away, along with unheard prayerful thanks.

# 34

# The Return

ONCE THE CARPETBAGGERS CLOSED THE BOMB BAY, the "Night Knight" high-tailed it out of there as it immediately increased its speed and altitude. Because they couldn't leave their posts, everyone on board had to simply congratulate himself silently as they climbed to a safer distance from enemy territory and continued their journey back to the base at Harrington. They were then able to hoot and holler as they celebrated their success in the mission.

But it wasn't over yet. They had been warned about the dangers of both take-offs and landings on missions such as this. While they made it to their target and completed their drop, they still had to travel back to the base with a limited amount of fuel.

After flying for many hours, pastel streaks of light blue were painted across the morning sky as they began their final approach to Harrington Field. They were able to spot the green light being flashed from the tower, indicating that the runway was clear. Bob remembered, "Our pilot brought that big black plane down as smooth as a whistle, and we were home! Now it was 'Mission Accomplished!'"

It didn't take them long to jump out of their posts and start congratulating each other. They had their first secret mission under their belts, and they were proud!

As they left the plane, they were immediately shuttled to headquarters, where Lt. Col. Fish and several other officers were waiting for them. After a round of congratulations from them, as usual, the crew was seated around a table set with glasses and the customary bottles of cognac. They were encouraged to drink to their success and to tell the officers everything they had witnessed during the mission that could help in assessing the location or strength of the enemy. Finally, they were de-briefed with a stern warning not to talk to anyone about their mission.

Then they were sent to the building where they had been dressed, and were allowed to change back to their more comfortable clothing. After that, they were off to the Mess Hall where they voraciously consumed large quantities of bacon and eggs—as Bob remarked, "...real eggs, not the powdered ones. And they were delicious!"

At last, they headed to their tents, exhausted, yet very happy. It didn't take long for all of those young Carpetbaggers to fall into deep slumber. One can only imagine their dreams.

# 35

# Blankets and Birds

M ID-DECEMBER, 1944. THE GERMAN ARMY had been secretly planning an attack on the Allied forces in the heavily-forested area of the Ardennes mountains on the western front (France, Belgium, and the Netherlands.) The Allies were preoccupied with plans of their own for an attack, and failed to act upon an intercepted message regarding the German offense. As a result, The Battle of the Bulge (so called due to the irregular shape of the German front line,) began on December 16, when the Allied forces were both surprised and unprepared for the overwhelming attack they suffered. The Allies' best planes were grounded by heavy overcast conditions, while the Germans were already in the air. It was the largest and bloodiest battle for the U.S. troops and they suffered more casualties than any other time in the war. [1]

Due to the loss of so many American soldiers, their ranks were integrated for the first time by U.S. President Dwight D. Eisenhower. Over 2,000 black soldiers had volunteered to go to the front, and by the end of World War II, 708 black Americans had died in combat.[2]

In mid-January, 1945, conditions were nearly unbearable with the severe winter cold (twenty degrees below zero,) and snow. The Allied troops were freezing and many were sick. Near the end of the battle, Bob Holmstrom and his Carpetbagger crew were ordered to fly supplies to them. The "Night Knight" had been loaded with a variety of items that were badly needed, including warm clothing, boots, socks, medical supplies, food, and blankets. Bob said, "Those guys were really suffering. We all gave half of our blankets to them."

They took off in the darkness, as always, and flew toward the area they had been assigned.

"As we approached, flares were being shot up into the sky. Bullets were flying all over the place," Bob recalled. "There was canon fire and machine gun tracer bullets. Searchlights lit the sky and the ground so we could spot troops in lines that varied from approximately one hundred miles long to twenty miles wide. The Germans were on one side, and on the other side were the Americans, along with the Canadians, French and British. Everything was lit up so bright, it was like the biggest Fourth of July display I ever saw in my life!

"It was an extremely treacherous situation to be in with fire from other planes in the sky and fire from the ground. There was even the possibility of 'friendly fire' from our own troops since our plane was black and pretty much unrecognizable in the night sky. Amazingly, we were able to deliver the supplies. Our plane had some damage, but we were able to fly it back to Harrington. We were just so lucky to drop our load and get out of there!"

A couple of months later, Bob Holmstrom and his crew were assigned to another important mission. This time they were to fly over the Ruhr River in Germany and release pigeons. The pigeons were of the "homing" breed and had been trained by people known as "pigeoneers" to return back to their home loft after their release, which could be an extraordinary distance. Some could actually fly as far as 600 miles. Their purpose was to bring back an important message regarding the location or movement of enemy forces or that of downed soldiers or sailors.[3]

More than two centuries ago, pigeons were used by the Roman Army in this manner. The birds have been proven quite reliable and have saved many lives over time. In early 1945, information concerning the precise location of the Axis forces and the direction they were heading was critical. MI-6 and the OSS agreed to the use of pigeons to obtain details instead of using radios that could alert the enemy.

Once again, Bob and his crew of the "Night Knight" rose into the deep blackness of the sky, this time with an unusual cargo to deliver. The area designated for the drop was in a valley where radio contact was poor. Ten Quaker oatmeal boxes had been carefully packed with a pigeon in each one, along with three days of food. Each bird had a small capsule attached to one of its legs. Inside the capsule was a small pencil and a piece of paper on which a message could be written. On each box was a small white parachute with a barometric fuse set to open the chute at an altitude so the box would land safely without harming the bird inside.

Bob will never forget that drop:

> *We had been following the river, which was curvy. It was an exhausting flight for the pilot. We were flying below 500 feet. Before we approached the target, I had to leave my position in the tail of the plane since I was assigned the job of releasing the containers. There were safety straps attached to both sides of the fuselage. The other ends of those straps were then attached to my parachute harness so I wouldn't fall out when I opened the rear bottom hatch.*

When we were nearing the drop zone, I pulled the hatch door open and the waist gunner handed me the first box. I wished the little guy inside luck and sent it sailing off into the night over Germany. I quickly repeated that procedure several more times before the pilot for some reason banked the plane ninety degrees. I was then sideways, with my head in the hatch, and I was looking up at a castle in the dark! We were flying below castles...obviously, the danger was extreme!

Well, I pulled myself inside and we avoided a crash. Later that morning, were we ever happy to see the White Cliffs of Dover, which we always viewed as the gate to our base!

We heard that several of the pigeons made it back to OSS/SOE headquarters in London.

That was our eighteenth mission and we soon did one more like it.

## 36

# Heroes of the Night

B
OB HOLMSTROM AND HIS CARPETBAGGER crewmates continued
to fly their missions of mercy to the resistance for many
months. The fact that they could only fly at low altitude on
moonlit nights with no lights on their big black B-24J made their
missions harrowing. Other aircraft in combat did not have to operate
under those restrictions. The secret missions required much from a
crew, always testing the boundaries of their skill and nerves. There
were many from other Carpetbagger crews who simply could not
stand the stress, and like the original copilot of Bob's crew, they
had to be reassigned.

The ones who remained, doggedly stuck to their routines and
continued to perform their jobs to the best of their abilities. Their
missions became further away and they frequently took fire from
guns on the ground, anti-aircraft missiles, or enemy planes. Many
were shot down, with some crew members able to escape by
parachute. But one had to wonder to what end, as it was likely
that they would either be killed or injured on impact, or taken
prisoner, in which case, the "L" pill was often the choice. Suicide

was generally preferable to capture, which would likely involve torture prior to certain death thereafter.

As their missions continued, Bob devised a secret code of his own to inform his girlfriend and family of the number he had completed. He said, "I would write 'Be sure to wish my sister a Happy Birthday. I can't believe she is eighteen already!' which would let them know that I had completed my eighteenth mission."

They flew a dozen more missions, dropping clothing and supplies to the resistance in Czechoslovakia and Germany. Once they flew very close to Hitler's mountain retreat, known as the "Eagle's Nest."

"On some of our missions, you could see a hundred miles," Bob recalled. "You could see Switzerland, lit up like New York City. When we flew over Dresden, the British had dropped incendiaries and the whole town was on fire. Sometimes the weather was brutal, and the Carpetbagger planes were the only ones who could get up to drop medicine and ammo to our troops, and there was a lot of rifle fire from the ground."

The Carpetbaggers always flew alone, never with an escort or any other plane. Sometimes there were spies who were boarded in the last minutes before takeoff. They were brought out to the runway by jeep and transferred into the plane through the bomb bay. The crew was forbidden to speak to them and vice versa. Usually they were men, but occasionally a female was with them. They were forced to sit on the floor during the flight, which Bob knew was most uncomfortable. When they finally arrived at his or her target zone, the "Joe Hole" was opened, and they each had to take his or her turn sitting on the edge of the opening high above the ground, then slide out through the hole into the dark of night. It had to be an incredible act of bravery! Once in a while, however, one of them would "need a nudge."

These people were agents and spies from the OSS, being sent

to carry out covert missions behind enemy lines. They and the Carpetbagger crews put their lives on the line with their unquestionable bravery and incredible skills.

It was rare for a Carpetbagger plane to return unscathed to Harrington following a mission. Most were peppered with bullet holes and gaping flak wounds. It is a tribute to the ground crews who spent many hours repairing and replacing damaged parts and patching the sides of the aircraft as best as they could with the diminishing stock of metal that they had to work with. When they got desperate, they raided the Mess Hall trash, foraging for tin cans to be cut and used as patches.

Following the allied invasion of Europe and the liberation of most of France, the necessity for Carpetbagger missions diminished, and they ended in May of 1945 after Bob and his crew had flown thirty successful missions in total.

Bob Holmstrom and his crew had been told early on that "If you survive three missions, you're lucky!" They were beyond "lucky." Bob recalled the many times they returned from missions with the plane full of holes from bullets or shrapnel and the ground crew marveling, "We can't figure out how nobody got hit!"

With unparalleled skill and bravery, those young men had become "heroes of the night."

# 37

# The Tide Turns

T HERE HAD BEEN SO MANY YEARS OF FIGHTING on both the Pacific and the European fronts; so many people ruthlessly tortured, seriously injured, or killed during the battles leading up to and including World War II. The statistics are unbelievably shocking, yet they are factual, and it is a horrific legacy of the four men who instigated the wars in the first place. Worldwide casualty totals are difficult to ascertain due to variations in the manner in which such information was gathered by the multitude of countries involved. An estimated sixty to one hundred million people suffered and died as a result of those wars.[1]

By June of 1945, Bob Holmstrom had finished his tour of duty in Europe. Two of the most brutal dictators in history had been defeated by the Allied Forces—and they were dead.

• Benito Mussolini's dreams of creating a large empire encompassing the Mediterranean with himself as emperor were crumbling. His military power had been overwhelmed. Any common sense he had was overshadowed by his megalomania.

The Italian people lost tens of thousands in a war of which they had wanted no part. In April 18, 1945, with the Allied forces moving into Italy, Mussolini and his mistress Claretta Petacci tried to escape by traveling north where they joined a German caravan of soldiers and disguised themselves in Nazi uniforms. On April 27, they were discovered and captured by the Italian underground. The next day, they were both shot, and their bodies were hung upside down in a grisly display before thousands of people in a Milan plaza, then cut down and dragged through the streets. There was an obvious lack of regret at his death. The man who had promised the Italian people the glory of Rome had delivered only misery.[2]

• At the same time, Adolph Hitler was forced to concede that Germany was not going to win the war against the Allied Forces. The Soviet Army had pushed the German troops back into western Europe and Hitler was caught in the middle with the Allies closing in. Hitler married his girlfriend Eva Braun in a civil ceremony on April 29, 1945. The next day, he received word of Mussolini's execution. Then one of the most ruthless dictators the world has ever known—the man who was responsible for the atrocious deaths and inconceivable suffering of tens of millions of people, including more than twenty million in the Soviet Union and six million Jews in Europe, that same man was "afraid" of falling into the enemy's hands. Twenty-four hours after the death of Mussolini, one day after their wedding, Adolph Hitler and his new wife both committed suicide. On May 7, 1945, Germany surrendered unconditionally to the Allies.[3]

• Joseph Stalin, dictator of the Soviet Union, had conducted "a reign of terror" over many years, as millions died from forced labor or starvation. By 1944, the tide had turned and the Soviet

Army was working against Hitler's forces by liberating countries in eastern Europe even before the Allies had mounted a serious challenge against Hitler at D-Day. The Red Army was also instrumental in liberating many survivors of the Nazi concentration camps. Stalin industrialized the U.S.S.R. with success, but the price paid was millions more deaths and serious environmental damage.[4]

Stalin would die of a stroke less than a decade later, on March 5, 1953, and the BBC reported, "Many in the Soviet Union mourn the loss of the leader who transformed the Soviet Union from a feudal economy to an industrialist power and played a critical role in defeating Hitler. But the millions incarcerated cheer at the demise of one of the most murderous dictators in history."[5]

• Only one of the four who began the wars that touched nearly every country in the world would remain after the death of Stalin—Emperor Hirohito. Hirohito would repudiate the traditional quasi-divine status of Japan's emperors on January 1, 1946. Japan would become a constitutional monarchy and Hirohito's powers would be severely limited.[6] The Japanese Emperor Hirohito did nothing to prevent the deaths and interminable suffering of millions of people at the hands of his country's Imperial Army.[7] Hirohito would live to witness the fury of the United States unleashed upon his country after the Japanese attack on Pearl Harbor and their continued aggression in the Pacific throughout World War II.

## 38

# Sworn to Secrecy

WHEN THE CARPETBAGGER MISSIONS ENDED, Bob Holmstrom's crew was assigned to other types of missions. V-E Day had occurred on May 8, 1945 when victory in Europe was publicly proclaimed, announcing Nazi Germany's acceptance of unconditional surrender in defeat by the Allied powers. However, in the wake of the war, there were many who needed to be rescued from stalags, concentration camps, and POW camps, plus some of our military men who had found a way to survive in the forests or the underground.

After they had flown twenty-five Carpetbagger missions in the dark, the war was coming to an end. However, Bob and his crew continued to fly medical supplies to the remaining troops and many other items so badly needed by Jewish people in stalags, and well as others in camps or those in the underground.

Following those extra missions, Bob and his crewmates received orders to return to the "Zone of the Interior," (the United States). But first, they were told to report to Headquarters. "The ten of us were escorted to a private room, where we waited for Lt. Col. Fish," said Bob. "When he entered, we all stood to salute

Bob (*rear, 4th from left*) and crew
prior to leaving Harrington AFB

Bob (*front left*) and two crewmates
form a victory pyramid

him, and before we sat down, he said, 'Raise your right hand,'
and we did so." Then he said, 'Swear that you will never disclose
anything you saw or did over here for the next forty years!' We
did as we were ordered."

He reiterated the consequences of breaking that oath, then
thanked them for their service and bid them farewell. If any of
them wondered why their missions had to remain secret for so
long, no one asked. Bob stated, "They didn't need to give us a
reason. We did not have to sign anything."

Proud of their service, the ten buddies headed back to their
tents to pack up their things.

They were going home!

# 39

# Homeward Bound

T HERE WAS A FLURRY OF ACTIVITY ON THE Harrington base
in May of 1945 as the U.S. Army Air Corps packed up to
leave. And there was a mixture of emotions as well. Bob
Holmstrom believed all of his crewmates probably felt the same
as he did. There was a reluctance to leave the place that had been
their shelter and their home. They were truly a "band of brothers."
Bob commented, "We had become a family with deep care and
concern for each of the others. We knew we would be separated
once we reached the States, but we vowed to keep in touch."

In addition to the separation anxiety they were experiencing,
there was also a sense of pride in the covert missions they had
been chosen to do, and the fact that they had survived so many
of those dangerous missions. And then, of course, there was
excitement in returning to their homes and families.

Bob and the members of his crew had breakfast at the Mess
Hall, then spent the morning packing their things and returning
war-related items that belonged to the military. Everything had
to be checked out of course, and there were long lines of guys
waiting for that process. The afternoon was spent preparing for

their flight out of Harrington. This included dressing properly, which they had grown accustomed to after that many missions, but it did take a while.

The weather that day was bad—heavy rain and wind— but Bob's crew was used to flying in more adverse conditions than most others were. As they walked out to that runway for the last time, there it was, waiting for them once again—"The Night Knight," their B-24J in all its glory, with its wounds patched up and ready to go again. They all took turns spinning the props, then boarded and took their positions for takeoff. The routine was second nature to them by now.

There were many planes lined up ahead of them, so it was a while before they were cleared. When they finally got the go-ahead, their plane rumbled down that runway, as they had done so many times before, with Bob and three other crewmates, in addition to ten ground crew on the floor, then they lifted off and once again just missed the trees at the end of the runway! (Perhaps due to the fact that the trees were shorter since planes had been "trimming them" for many months.)

Their plane was heavily loaded with items to be returned to the U.S. After takeoff, Bob and the others on the floor took their positions as they headed for Preswick, Scotland, buffeted by more heavy rain and wind. Upon landing, and with the weight of their cargo, a tire blew and the aircraft "went loco." "We were all over that runway!" Bob remembered. Nonetheless, their skilled pilot as he had always done, gained control and they were safe.

They spent the night at the Preswick base, then began their trek over the "Big Pond." Leaving Europe the next morning in their own plane, Bob and his crewmates headed to Reykjavik, Iceland. The crew was delighted to see Quonset huts, where they spent the night. Bob remarked, "The people in Iceland were all blonde, both men and women. And I never saw so many gray rocks in my life!"

The next morning, they were off to Goose Bay, Labrador. From there, they flew down to Bradley Field, Connecticut, where they went through customs and handed over any extra guns.

# 40

# Final Countdown
# in the Pacific

THE JAPANESE IMPERIAL ARMY HAD experienced great success by 1945. After decimating the U.S. Pacific fleet at Pearl Harbor four years earlier, they had removed the biggest obstacle in their path to enlarging their empire by attacking, ravaging, and occupying many other countries, territories in the Far East, and islands in the Pacific.

Under the leadership of U.S. General Douglas MacArthur, who was appointed commander of the Southwest Pacific Theater by FDR on March 18, 1942, and Admiral Chester Nimitz, who was named Commander-in-Chief of the U.S. Pacific Theater on March 24, 1942, many battles were fought with the U.S. and Allied forces attempting to squelch the relentless Japanese offense.[1]

There were innumerable other battles, proving that the Japanese Imperial Army had no intention of slowing down. In fact, they originated Kamikaze (suicide) attacks against U.S. warships in the Leyte Gulf on October 25,1944. Two months later, the U.S. began preparations to finally stop them.[2]

Harry S. Truman became President of the United States upon the death of Franklin D. Roosevelt on April 12, 1945. Shortly after, on May 8th, 1945, VE Day (Victory in Europe) was finally declared and countries around the world celebrated enormously.[3]

Meanwhile, there was still the war with Japan to be dealt with. The Manhattan Project, with collaboration from Canada and the U.K., had been originated by FDR. It was top-secret, involving the development of atomic weapons, and they were ready to test the first nuclear weapon, which was accomplished on July 16 of 1945 in New Mexico.[4]

The "Potsdam Declaration" that called for the surrender of all Japanese armed forces was issued by the United States, the U.K., and China on July 26, 1945. The ultimatum stated that if Japan did not surrender, it would face prompt and utter destruction. There was no response from Japan.[5]

As a result, the first atomic bomb (code-named "Little Boy") was dropped on the Japanese city of Hiroshima on August 6, 1945, and three days later, a second one (code-named "Fat Man") was dropped on the city of Nagasaki. Both cities and their populations were devastated.[6]

Emperor Hirohito finally accepted the Potsdam Declaration and its terms on August 15, 1945. He signed the surrender documents on board the USS *Missouri* on September 2, 1945, as 1,000 U.S. carrier-based planes flew overhead and President Harry Truman declared VJ Day (Victory in Japan). This was followed by a radio announcement from Hirohito to the Japanese people. It was the first time many of them had ever heard the voice of their Emperor.[7]

Many people believed that Hirohito should have been tried as a war criminal, but General MacArthur was in favor of retaining stability by implementing a new Japanese constitution that included denouncing imperial "divinity." Hirohito reluctantly agreed and as a result, his powers were severely curtailed.[8] He would die of cancer at the age of eighty-eight on January 7, 1989.[9]

# 41

# Moving On

T HROUGHOUT HIS TRAINING IN THE United States and in the U.K., followed by his many missions as a Carpetbagger, one thought was always with Bob Holmstrom. He had time to think about what he was going to do with his life after he was discharged from the service. Foremost on his "To Do List," was to resume his relationship with his "galfriend" Lorraine Heyn. He was definitely looking forward to seeing her again soon.

Bob had been granted a thirty-day leave. It was his first leave in ten months (since being shipped overseas.) He was sent from Bradley Field, Connecticut, to Fort McCoy in Wisconsin by train. It was a passenger train and he actually got a seat on it, which was a welcome surprise. After a short time at Fort McCoy, he boarded another train. That one was headed for the St. Paul, Minnesota Depot, and he was on his way home!

Bob Holmstrom was a different person than the boy who had left. He had trained and learned many skills so proficiently that he was one of a select few carefully chosen to participate in dangerous clandestine missions and help win the war. He had seen some terrible things with crashes of planes carrying people he knew, or the empty beds of those who never returned. His plane had taken plenty of anti-aircraft, ground, and direct fire while he served as a tail gunner on that big B-24J Liberator. He was an integral part of the secret Carpetbagger missions. He had met many people, from his crewmates to many others on the bases and towns along the way, in addition to the several officers he answered to and admired. He had been part of a campaign to assist the desperate people of the resistance. He wore his uniform with great pride. He had become a man.

# 42

# The Homecoming and a Trip Downtown

I N LESS THAN TWO HOURS AFTER THE TRAIN left near the Fort McCoy Army base in Wisconsin, it was about to pull into the depot in St. Paul, Minnesota. An excited Bob Holmstrom was aboard. He had been away for ten months and now had a deeper appreciation for all that life can offer, and he planned to make the most of his own life after risking it to serve and save others during the war. As they entered the station, Bob scanned the waiting crowd for the faces he was anxious to see, but many people were gathered on the platform, and he couldn't spot the ones he was looking for. So he gathered his things and proceeded down the narrow aisle between the seats, heading for the open door at the end of the car he was in. When he reached the exit, he paused in the opening, scanning the group on his right. With no sight of his family, he was forced to step down. But just as his feet touched the platform, he heard his name called, coming from the left side. And there she was.

Lorraine Heyn was there to greet him with a hug, and boy, was he happy to see her! His mom and dad, along with his sister and Lorraine's parents were there as well. After their greetings, they all left to go home. The Holmstroms rode in one car, while Bob got to ride with the Heyns. He held Lorraine's hand all the way there before they dropped him off at his house.

Lorraine had three sisters, Dolores, Yvonne, and Dianne. Since her parents, Bill and Elizabeth, never had a son, they had pretty much "adopted" Bob as their own, and he said they were "just great" to him. They treated him with kindness and respect. Bob admitted that he "had a better relationship with them than he ever did with his own family." During his leave, he enjoyed fishing with Bill Heyn. Bob and Lorraine spent time swimming in Lake Phalen, going to movies, out for lunch, and sharing their feelings about one another.

Asked when he first got serious about Lorraine, Bob quickly responded with a grin, "Oh, I think we were serious pretty much right away! She was cute and we just really liked the same things."

It was no surprise when Bob approached her father one day and asked for his daughter's hand in marriage. Bill Heyn's response was immediate: "Yes! Take her—and take care of her!"

From there, Bob went to the living room, where he proposed to Lorraine, (whom he had started to call "Rain," since her mother said she had been born on a day with incessant heavy rainfall.) She happily accepted, and her sister, Yvonne, who had witnessed the scene, scurried off to tell the rest of the family.

Bob recalled, "Males under the age of twenty-one needed a permit from their parents to marry. I was twenty and my parents gave written permission without hesitation. Rain was eighteen and did not need parental permission. We were engaged but my leave was up and I had to return to Ft. McCoy."

On August 24, 1945, Bob was home again on a short leave. He

and Rain went by themselves to the Justice of the Peace in St. Paul, Minnesota. With a smile, he recalled, "We asked the first people we saw who were walking down the hall if they would be witnesses to our marriage, and they agreed. Justice John D. O'Donnell performed the ceremony. Then we took the streetcar downtown and checked into the St. Paul Hotel. That evening, we went to a restaurant called Nu Ken Chu, where we enjoyed a dinner of Chow-Mein (with cashews on top.) Afterwards, we went back to the hotel where we spent the night."

Bob continued, this time with no smile:

*I made a promise to myself that I shared with Rain: I would never go hungry again, as I had during most of my childhood, and that when we had children I would never treat them the way I had been treated as a child....Rain was working as a dental assistant, and we stayed at her parents' house. They were the best in the world. But then I had to leave her again.*

She said, "Yes!"

# 43

# A Good Deal,
# Then Time to Go

Soon after his wedding ceremony, Bob was on the train again, returning to Fort McCoy in Wisconsin. He wasn't there long before he was sent to Sioux Falls, South Dakota. He said, "I was there about thirty days while they were deciding what to do with us. There was talk that we may be sent to Japan. Because I was short two points from getting out, it was likely that I would be sent there. So I was trying to learn a little Japanese."

One day, an officer came around, asking if anyone could type on an electric typewriter. Bob answered that he could. There was an opening in Fort Dix, New Jersey, for a manager of an office of twenty people and the CO was a major. Bob was soon on his way out east. He enjoyed working in the office there, mostly typing discharge papers for Women in the Air Corps (WACs), and there were benefits he had never expected. First, the CO got everyone in his office into the Officers' Mess Hall. "It was a real privilege," declared Bob. Then he got even better news. "We were told that we could live on the base or in town. I called my wife, and she was quickly on a train to New Jersey—and the government paid her way there!"

During the two and a half months that Bob worked at Fort Dix, he and Rain were able to do "lots of sight-seeing" up and down the east coast. Traveling by train, they visited the Radio City Theater in New York City, where they saw Frank Sinatra perform. They explored other towns and tourist locations as well. In Philadelphia, by chance, Bob met his godmother's son, Gary. They had not seen each other in years, but still recognized one another. He was in full Navy uniform, and they had an interesting exchange about their military service, though Bob could not reveal details of his own.

On December 18, 1945, Bob was formally discharged from the service. Mr. and Mrs. Robert Holmstrom happily made it home for Christmas.

Bob and his wife, Rain, home at last

# 44

# Home Sweet Home Upstairs

B OB AND RAIN HAD MUCH TO CELEBRATE that Christmas. He had proudly and safely carried out his duty, in spite of the dangers he had faced with the Carpetbagger missions. Also, they had a place to live. His father-in-law had offered them an upstairs room. There was no heat in there and it wasn't insulated, so a neighbor who was a handyman, installed a gas line and a small heater, which kept them comfortable enough in the winter of 1946. But in the summer, it was a different story. Bob declared, "It was so hot in that room, you could roast a turkey up there!"

He went back to work for Swift and Company, where he had been employed during his high school years, and he did the same job of meat packing. Rain was soon pregnant and didn't have to work, because Bob was making enough to support them while living with her parents. They stayed there for two and a half years.

In April of 1946, Swift went on strike, and Bob would not be working for a while. His father-in-law was employed as a tile setter for Drake Marble and Tile, and there happened to be an opening at that time. Bob never went back to work at Swift. He became a tile setter instead. He said, "I learned what I could from Bill, and I had a friend who did fancy tile work, who taught me the artistic side of the job. I took classes at a vocational school and got a teacher's degree in tile setting. I was one of only three in the state then."

Six months later, on October 3, 1946, Bob became a father when Rain delivered a baby boy, and they named him Robert Eugene Holmstrom, Jr.

Bob had been working on some major tile jobs at hospitals in metropolitan Minneapolis and St. Paul, Minnesota, including the Schmidt and Hamm's breweries. He also did tile work in all of the Duluth, Minnesota, hospitals at that time.

# 45

# Fast Forward, Then Stop

A DECADE LATER, BOB'S FAMILY WAS about to grow. Rain was pregnant again, and on February 20, 1956, a daughter was born. They named her Jennifer Lee.

Bob's tile-setting business was taking him farther away from Minnesota. He was driving to North Dakota and Montana where he got plenty of work. Over the years, as his children grew, the family would travel with him in the summer months and they visited Yellowstone National Park several times.

He had put plenty of miles on his car before he came to a standstill in 1962. Bob, Rain, and Jennifer were in the family's Plymouth Signet convertible near Duluth, Minnesota, with seventeen-year-old Robert, Jr. behind the wheel. They were at a stop sign, when he looked in the rear-view mirror and suddenly shouted, "We're gonna get hit!" They were rear-ended. Both Bob and Rain were injured. Thankfully, they were all wearing seatbelts and the children were not hurt, but they were all taken to St. Mary's Hospital, where Bob and Rain were both treated for whiplash injuries. They were hospitalized for three days, while Robert, Jr. and Jennifer were taken by relatives to Two Harbors, Minnesota.

Bob's whiplash injury was finally improving when one day he was driving a '64 Volkswagen in Minneapolis, Minnesota. He was hit by a Ford T-Bird. Bob's neck was re-injured. "It didn't break my neck, but left it sitting on the shoulder bone," he recalled. "I spent the next six months in traction and therapy, and I could not work." Even after spending that much time in the hospital, he was unable to bend his neck in order to hold his head upward for any length of time. "It screwed up my tile-setting, especially ceilings. Insurance in those days was not good. With little income, we had to use our savings just to pay our living expenses."

# 46

# Back in Uniform

IT WAS APPARENT THAT BOB NEEDED TO seek alternative employment following the neck injuries he had sustained in the two automobile accidents, as well as additional employment to fill the economic hole he was in after having to spend six months in the hospital. His savings had been wiped out as he paid his medical bills, and he had to declare bankruptcy. It was most unfortunate and through no fault of his own, he was left in dire circumstances.

However, like the true soldier he was, as soon as his strength allowed, Bob was "pounding the pavement," seeking any kind of work he could get. Soon he was working three different jobs. He did some basic tile setting for the Northwestern Tile Company, and he worked as a security guard for the Knox Lumber Company. In 1959, he applied to the Police Department in North St. Paul, Minnesota. He was hired as a police officer, and was back in uniform (although this one lacked wings.)

Even with that many jobs, it would take years to recover from his debt, but Bob Holmstrom was determined to pay back every penny. "It wasn't easy," he said. "For ten years I scheduled three work

Bob in St. Paul, Minnesota

shifts, and my family lived on a shoestring during that time, but we did ok. Eventually I paid all my debts. We recovered and life was good again."

The following year, Northwest Airlines was building a new hangar at the airport in Minneapolis, Minnesota, and they were hiring new employees. Tired of working nights patrolling the streets of North St. Paul, Bob applied for a job with the airline. When he learned that the pay was better than he had been making, it was an easy choice for him. They offered him a position as a security officer. He was still in uniform, although his badge no longer read "Police" but now "Security."

The Holmstrom family (*left to right*): Robert, Jr.,
Bob, Rain, and Jennifer

Bob enjoyed his work at the airport and he was number two
on the seniority list, which provided a measure of job security
over the years. Bob commented, "It was a small, private police
department, and we drove squad cars."

Working for the airline brought special benefits in the form of
discount airfare for Bob and his family members. He got his first
pass and his first flight on a commercial plane. He liked it. He
and Rain flew down to Miami, where he said it was "brutally
hot." In addition to the money-saving flight, they received 50%
off hotels as well.

When they checked into the beachfront hotel, they happened
to meet the owner, who was a kind Jewish man, and after a brief
conversation, he offered them a room on the ocean and invited
them for drinks later that day.

From then on, when Minnesota would play football against
Miami, if Bob and Rain could get away, they would fly down

there, and "get tickets cheap." And their friend, the hotel owner, would meet them with a limousine.

Over the years, Bob and his family got to travel all over the United States, including Hawaii. He and Rain enjoyed several cruises to Mexico and the Caribbean. After twenty-two years of working for Northwest Airlines, at the age of sixty-two, Bob retired.

He and Rain enjoyed camping and eventually they purchased a large motorhome with which they made many happy memories.

# A Vision Realized

WILLIAM J. DONOVAN HAD CREATED AN "OSS empire" by late 1944, with spies and secret agents from all walks of life and every branch of the military. As many as 13,000 people were imbedded in countries all over the world. The massive organization he created was critical in helping the Allies to win World War II in both the European and Asian theaters by gathering secret intelligence, conducting guerilla warfare and propaganda war against the enemy, creating new technology, performing acts of sabotage, and sending thousands of OSS representatives (such as the Carpetbaggers) into enemy territory on some of the most dangerous missions of the war.[1]

In the fall of 1945, Bill Donovan's OSS air crews were assisting in locating downed pilots and missing agents in Germany.[2] Yet, his Office of Strategic Services, for the most part, was still considered a "rogue agency" by his many opponents and his British partners as well. "Wild Bill" had ridden a proverbial "bucking bronco" throughout the war, charging forth, refusing to give up. Against the bureaucracy, he fiercely defended the agency he created; however, when the war finally ended, the Office of

Strategic Services would soon end as well, along with many other war agencies.

On April 12, 1945, President Franklin D. Roosevelt was at his beloved sanctuary in Warm Springs, Georgia, where he died from a massive cerebral hemorrhage. After twelve years in the White House, he was succeeded by Vice President Harry S. Truman.[3]

Harry S. Truman was "not fond of Donovan." In September of that year he signed executive Order 9621, terminating the OSS, effective October 1, 1945.

Its functions were split between the State and War Departments.[4]

Bill Donovan resumed his law practice, but he never gave up on his conviction concerning the necessity of a central intelligence agency in the United States. He continued to push that agenda with characteristic unbridled passion, and by 1947, President Truman began to realize the value of centralizing intelligence in the interest of national security.

After finally listening to advice from Donovan and Admiral William D. Leahy, Truman established the Central Intelligence Group (CIG) in January, 1946.[5]

One year later, under provisions of the National Security Act of 1947, both the National Security Council (NSC) and the Central Intelligence Agency (CIA) were created. on July 26, 1947.[6] The new CIA was a vindication of Donovan's vision.[7]

## 48

# Hidden Treasure

A S THE YEARS PASSED, ONE DAY IN THE FALL of 1993, Bob's daughter Jenny was visiting her grandmother at her home in St. Paul. This was the house where her mother had grown up, and Jenny knew it well.

After enjoying lunch together and a good deal of conversation on that fall afternoon, Jenny's grandmother asked her if she would help to clean out the closet upstairs. Her husband Bill had passed away and she wanted to be sure that nothing was left up there.

A carpeted staircase led to the second floor. The closet was just an area that was under the slant of the roof, and it was a tight space. They both got in and began to collect all of the items that were left there and carried them downstairs.

They were about to call it quits when Jenny took one last glance around. In a far corner, a piece of insulation had fallen from the ceiling and landed on top of something they had missed. When her grandmother was downstairs, Jenny cleared away some of the insulation. A few old boxes which had been preserved, but forgotten, were revealed. When her grandmother returned, Jenny asked her what might be in those boxes, but she was told, "Oh, it's probably some of Dianne's old books, so just carry them downstairs. Get them out of here and give them to the Goodwill." Jenny took them out to her car.

When she got home, she decided to take the boxes from her trunk and put them in her living room so she could open them to determine what their contents were. When she opened the flaps on the top of the first box, she stared into it, and caught her breath. It took a moment for her to process what it was that she had discovered. The boxes contained her dad's war memorabilia.

Jenny immediately called her parents, only to find that her dad had gone hunting up north and wouldn't be home for a couple of days. Disappointed that he wasn't there, Jenny told her mother that she was coming to her house anyway with "something of interest." Soon she was carrying the boxes into their kitchen, and she placed them on the table. Then she told her mother to open them. Rain was stunned by what she saw. Bob had lost track of those boxes many years ago. A robbery had taken place in a house where they once lived and he thought they had been stolen from there.

Jenny and her mother took just about everything out of the boxes and looked in amazement at some of the items inside. When they came to the letters Bob had written to Rain, Jenny admitted that she had read a few of them. Rain responded with, "That is personal mail. Nobody should be reading them but me!" She also commented that, "If your dad does not get emotional when he opens those boxes, I'll eat my shoes!"

Apart from the "personal mail," Jenny and her mom had a few laughs and were intrigued by some of the items they discovered in the boxes. Two days later, Bob came home, and his wife and daughter were anxiously waiting for him with the big surprise. They led him to the kitchen and there were the boxes they had carefully re-packed. He did not recognize them at first.

They told Bob to go ahead and open them. When he opened

the first box, he gasped, just as Jenny had done. Then, filled with surprise and great happiness, Bob looked into the box containing the items he had brought back from the war. As he explored the items inside, a smile spread ear-to-ear across his face. Those things that he had assumed were lost forever were once more back in his hands, and they were treasure to him.

There were boxes within the boxes. Bob's medals were in one of them, and his eyes flooded when he saw them. (Happily, Rain did not have to "eat her shoes!") A cigar box was full of wartime silver dollars. There were pictures he had taken during the war. Many of the love letters and fancy pillowtop covers he had sent to Rain while he was overseas were preserved.

The other box contained mainly military items, including his first-aid kit, some button compasses, a downward-curved flashlight, a silk map of European territories, a gas mask, and parts of his uniform (which, he proudly declared, "still fit!")

As the family viewed the items once they had all been removed from the boxes, questions were asked, although Bob still did not divulge his wartime experience. It was not until he attended a Carpetbagger Reunion in 2006 where he learned that the details of their operations had been declassified a few years earlier. Well past the required forty years of sworn secrecy, Bob finally began to explain to his family what the OSS was and how they had assigned him to the covert special ops of the Carpetbagger missions. They were all stunned.

Jenny said, "Knowing that he had done such courageous things in the war helped us to understand why he is so smart and can fix anything. It also explains why he is such a good worker."

She added, "Most of all, it helped us to know who he is and why."

[*See Appendixes A-L for photos of Bob's memorabilia.*]

# 49

# A Helping Hand

AFTER HE RETIRED, BOB SPENT A GOOD AMOUNT of his time volunteering to help others. Years before, he had noticed that many children were hanging around the Margaret Street Playground in St. Paul with little to do. Bob started a Cub Scout group (#217) in 1947, which was still active more than seventy years later.

In 1983, he joined the American Legion in North St. Paul. He and Rain, along with eight others, regularly went to the VA Medical Center in Minneapolis, Minnesota where they would spend a few hours visiting others who had been in the service but had no one else to visit with them. They brought the veterans treats such as candy bars and cookies, as well as a variety of personal items including toothpaste, deodorant, brushes and combs, etc. They spent time with many of the vets and had pleasant conversations with them. "It meant a lot to them," Bob said.

Both Bob and Rain enjoyed the experience and took pleasure in volunteering their time in that way. Then the man who had introduced them to this kind of volunteer service, had to quit. So

Bob became the leader and served in that position for many years, coordinating the collection and distribution of items to be taken to the VA Medical Center. In time they expanded their efforts to two more locations in Minnesota: The VA Hospital in Hastings and the Veterans Home in Minneapolis.

"My post at the American Legion got interested in what I was doing," stated Bob. "They wanted to help, and they gave me a checking account and $1,000 dollars to start. Along the way, I met others who wanted to play a part. I got a call from the 'Veterans on the Lake' organization in Ely, Minnesota, and from the Metropolitan Recreation Director of Silver Bay, Minnesota, where my cousin served on the board." Those organizations helped with money or items collected for the veterans to be distributed by Bob and his team. Many people in all of the locations they serviced donated items, and sometimes there were as many as 500 items to give, (such as shoes, clothing, TVs, etc.) After many years, Bob handed over the leadership position to someone else, but he did not stop his regular schedule of visiting those organizations.

At the age of ninety-two, Bob's commitment to helping others was still going strong:

> In 2013, the 4th District American Legion organized a program called "Shop, Ship, and Share" to send boxes to the troops during the holidays. In early December, the Maplewood Mall in Minnesota provides a large area for us on their lower level from which we warehouse, organize, and ship our boxes. We sponsor drives throughout the metropolitan area to collect all sorts of items and cards our troops might enjoy. I collected 150 pounds of candy myself the other day. Then at least thirty people and I work for

*two days filling boxes. We have been doing this since 2013. An average estimate is 1,100 to 1,200 boxes ready to be shipped out all over the world every year in time for the upcoming holidays. It's a program I am proud to be a part of.*

In order to visit or volunteer at a VA hospital, one must obtain clearance, including fingerprints and a background check, which Bob and Rain had done many years ago. Together, they made more than 1,000 little American flags using small gold safety pins and red, white, and blue seed beads. The end result of an incredible number of hours on their part were beautiful little pins that are tiny movable flags to be worn proudly on the chest of everyone who received one from Bob and his wife.

Rain spent many hours repairing clothing for veterans in the VA Homes and collecting puzzles, picture books, and personal items for them.

Lorraine received the Unit Member of the Year Award for 2007-08 from the Minnesota American Legion Auxiliary. It rewarded both her and Bob with an all-expenses-paid trip to a resort in Phoenix. It included air, hotels, and meals. They were transported by limousine to and from the airport and given the use of a convertible while there.

After their return, the City of St. Paul hosted a parade for Rain, and she rode through the streets in a convertible.

Bob stated, "She was a real partner." Those who knew them well said, "Where he was, she was."

After Rain passed away in 2013, Bob continued to faithfully visit the VA Hospital twice a month on Sundays. He was a member of the Eagles, Moose, and VFW, in addition to the American Legion. He was often in charge of the Retirement Group picnics for Northwest Airlines.

Bob and his beloved Rain

Bob visited several schools over the years, talking to students about his war experience, and he was invited to speak to other groups as well.

Helping others had been a desire of Bob Holmstrom since he was young, and throughout his life, he demonstrated that in numerous ways.

# 50

# Looking Back

AFTER LIVING MORE THAN NINETY-ONE YEARS, Bob Holmstrom one day reminisced about the life he lived. His childhood was definitely challenging. While Bob's family was quite poor, when he was young, Bob didn't realize it. He simply thought that they lived the same way as most others did. But their poverty created real problems for Bob. He was almost always hungry and the only toys he had were mainly things he could make himself. Christmas and birthdays only brought old clothes (his own or someone else's) with hems let down or seams enlarged. The fact that his father had to move frequently in order to find work was not only a hardship on the family, but for Bob in particular. By the time he started school, he was enrolled and disenrolled several times, which made his education a serious challenge, aside from the difficulty of maintaining friendships.

However, poverty was not the only adversity he faced while growing up. He was treated harshly by his father, and his mother failed to intervene. While he was provided with the basic essentials, he was denied any show of love or affection by either of his parents and they never told him that they loved him.

Young Bob was blessed with an inner strength and a good mind. Against the odds, he managed the difficulty of his circumstances and made the best of them. Some of his relatives provided random acts of kindness toward him and made him feel included. The influence of the church was significant in Bob's life as he enjoyed participating in its choirs, clubs, activities, and Boy Scouts who held their meetings there.

It became apparent early on in Bob's life that he was different from many others who would suffer far more from the effects of a lifestyle such as his. He studied hard and did quite well in school, and he got along with others, as he was shuffled back and forth from various homes on Minnesota's Iron Range to ten different homes in metropolitan St. Paul before he graduated from high school.

His relationship with a girl he called "Rain" had given him confidence and the warm acceptance by her and her parents was like nothing he had ever experienced with his own family.

Bob appreciated the structure of the military, in spite of the fact that he was often moved around there too. By then, he was more used to moving than the average recruit., and he enjoyed the opportunity to make new friends and to see new places. He found it interesting to observe how people lived differently as environments changed. He had decent clothes that fit and he got at least two square meals a day, plus a roof over his head without having to pay for room and board.

Excelling in several areas of his training, Bob did not go unnoticed by his instructors. He was one of a select few who were ultimately chosen to perform highly secret missions in collaboration with the Office of Selective Services. The missions required absolute secrecy and the top level of skill in the responsibilities of each young man who flew into the dark of night in order to deliver supplies and spies for the people of the resistance in war-torn countries such as Germany, Denmark, France, the Netherlands, Poland, and the Czech Republic. Those who agreed to be part of those secret missions, did so well-aware of the high level of risk to themselves. They were the "Carpetbaggers," and Bob Holmstrom was one of them.

As he reviewed his more than nine decades of life on this earth, Bob was pleased. He had always tried his best, in spite of the difficulties. He found the love of his life and enjoyed sixty-nine years of marriage with his beloved "Rain" and together they raised a son, Robert, Jr., and a daughter, Jennifer. In time, they had four grandchildren named Julie, Jerome, Mark, and Amanda.

As a young boy, Bob had wanted to help save others by becoming a doctor, but his life circumstances had prevented that from happening. However, through his participation in the Carpetbagger missions, he and the young men who flew with him had without a doubt, saved many lives and helped to shorten the deadliest war in history

After the war ended, the Carpetbaggers continued to fly several times on what were dubbed "mercy missions," which were primarily delivering medical supplies. Bob will always remember seeing large white-washed rocks along the coast of the Netherlands fifty feet above the water and stretching 300 feet, spelling out the words "THANKS, LIBERATORS!"

It has been said that a difficult childhood can break a person—or it can make one stronger. Clearly, it made Bob Holmstrom stronger.

The qualities that his Air Force instructors saw in him were the exact skills and traits they were seeking in the select few chosen to serve as Carpetbaggers. And they are many of the same traits that set Bob apart from the ordinary throughout his life as he continued to help other veterans.

After more than nine decades, a loving and faithful marriage of sixty-nine years, a son, a daughter, and four grandchildren, Bob was asked at the age of ninety-one what he felt is the most important thing in life. He immediately said family was first, followed by his service to his country. "As Carpetbaggers, we were there to help save lives, not to kill people," Bob said. " I am very proud to have been a part of those missions."

# Creative Deception

DECEPTION HAS BEEN USED DURING times of war for centuries. It takes many forms and is used to deceive the enemy. The ancient Trojan horse is an example. It has been employed to successfully win many wars. Over the years, strategies for tactical deception have evolved into realistic replicas of the real thing. It can be effective in luring an enemy into an ambush or to take action through the use of decoys, or false propaganda.

During the Civil War, fake cannons were produced by painting logs black and mounted on a stump. Called "Quaker guns," from a distance, they resembled an imposing threat.[1]

During World War II, it was the British who were quite advanced in the field of espionage, who influenced the U.S. military leaders to accept and successfully practice many of its secret weapons and techniques. By employing artists immediately upon graduation, and professionals, they were able to create very believable ruses, including faux uniforms, footprint molds on a stick (both barefoot and shoeless), and the ultimate in visual deception—inflatable Sherman tanks. By painting stripes in a pattern on a ship, detection was lessened, and civilians on the ground sometimes painted stripes on their animals so they could locate them during blackouts.[2]

There was also auditory deception. Sound systems attached to vehicles rolling along the front lines mimicked the sound of troops marching, and often worked to deceive the opposition. Also, false information was deliberately broadcast by radio operators to misguide their opponents.[3]

The OSS, under Colonel William Donovan, had invested considerably in the field of deception techniques, first by secret and double agents. A physician named Christian J. Lambertsen requested an appointment with Donovan to demonstrate some equipment that he had recently developed, but had been rejected by the Navy. Donovan was open to it since he was in the process of developing a maritime unit for the OSS. It happened that the device was beyond the dreams of even "Wild Bill" Donovan. He readily bought into it and it was soon assigned an acronym for Lambertsen's Self-Contained Underwater Breathing Apparatus—now known universally as SCUBA.[4]

In a quote attributed to Bill Donovan upon hiring Boston chemist Stanley Lovell, he said, "I need every subtle device and every underhanded trick to use against the Germans and the Japanese…You will have to invent all of them, Lovell, because you're going to be my man."[5]

Lovell had done his job, and he produced many things of crucial use to the agents, the people of the resistance, as well as the soldiers and crews of the ships and planes Donovan employed to conduct his empire of espionage. A few of Lovell's valuable creations were a miniature camera disguised as a matchbox, buttons with concealed compasses, exploding animal dung, and explosive powder hidden in bags of Chinese flour. However, his most famous invention was that of the pistol silencer.[6]

Stanley Lovell was Bill Donovan's version of James Bond's

"Q." His inventions were effectively used to shorten the conflict and reduce the losses.[7]

# 52

# "Secret Heroes Who Flew in the Night"

*Jennifer Nelson, daughter of Robert E. Holmstrom, is actively involved in the American Legion Auxiliary and was appointed Carpetbagger Coordinator in 2017, as the OSS and the Carpetbaggers organizations were united. She has beautifully preserved her dad's wartime photos in artful scrapbooks and his many medals in a large velvet-lined display case. Jennifer also wrote this heartfelt poem in honor of her father's service as a "Carpetbagger" during World War II.*

Long ago was a man, who was just 18; left home to win the war, or so it seemed.

Dreaming to be a pilot, at Harrington Field he would be; serving his country, so we could be free.

It was labeled the War to end all Wars; later to learn, there would be many more.

The training was fierce, the goal was unknown; how many months would he be away from home?

The OSS chose him as part of the crew; in the 406th, drop sites were unknown until they flew.

Who is this Carpetbagger who served in WW2? He is just a civilian who served people like me and you.

Pilots were expendable, to Morse code he said no. He chose to be a gunner, in hopes to exit safely through the Joe Hole.

Average life as a gunner was 12 seconds in combat; if you ditched down to sea, you'd freeze in 5 minutes flat.

At 30 below zero, they flew in the dark; with doors wide open, his mask left a deep mark.

To help out people but not to fight; this is why they could only fly in the night.

They dropped bicycles, clothes and sometimes a spy; these heroes never looked back to wonder why.

The Night Knight so fully loaded they scraped tops of trees; thank the Lord they made it - He came home to love you and me.

They depended on each other, they watched each other's back, with the danger of their mission, the sky was ever so black.

If one of the crew put them in harm's way; they pulled together or there would be hell to pay.

 Danger all around them, they never could see; they look back now to realize what they did just had to be.

30 successful missions on the B24; all these men wanted to do more.

No internet, cell phones, only postcards or a letter; took months to reach home, sooner would have been better.

Mom never knew where her guy would be; nor did she know the impact

or to what degree.

Two plus years later, the mission was closed; his life went on, still no one would know.

He was sworn to secrecy for 40 years; now decades later,
still many things we need to hear.

Grandma's attic is where they once lived - the treasures
of their past, they were hers and his.

He went through the pictures, named each of his crew;
then wondered who was alive, he wished he knew.

His metals and certificates he could finally prove; but
that was not his intention, he was just so moved.

Tears ran down his face; he realized what he had; these
things from the past were important to my Dad.

There were coins, maps, trinkets, and images of bombs;
but I cherish the love notes he wrote to my Mom.

In the last few years she's just realized; that the love of
her life was more than just wise.

I love to tell his story - one we all need to know; these
are the rare men, and if asked, would say, "When can I
go?"

I want you to know my Dad wanted to do things right;
and that is why he was chosen to fly Secret Missions in
the Night!

Jennifer Nelson and
her father, Robert
Eugene Holmstrom

# 53

# A Final Tribute to Donovan, the OSS, and the Carpetbaggers

WILLIAM J. DONOVAN BUILT A MASSIVE special operations organization that was called the Office of Strategic Services in 1942. With more than forty locations throughout the world, over 13,000 people were involved as staff members, secret agents, or spies. During World War II, he added an air division to his covert missions, and it was code-named "Operation Carpetbagger." The men and women who were part of these missions risked their lives to assist the people of enemy-occupied countries. Their secret operations were a closely-guarded secret for forty years, and since then, it is still largely unknown.

More than seven decades after World War II ended, Congress passed through both the House of Representatives and the Senate, an Act which awards the highest civilian honor for heroic acts of bravery. On March 21, 2018, in Washington, D.C. the Congressional Gold Medal was presented to the OSS and its Carpetbaggers for the heroic bravery and sacrifices of the men and women who worked

Major General William J. Donovan and his statue at CIA original headquarters, Langley, VA (Photos with permission of CIA.org)

for the covert organization and its extremely dangerous missions and to the many who did not survive.)

It is also in recognition of the contribution of Major General William Donovan and the men and women employed by him, whose efforts helped to win and shorten the war. William J. Donovan is now considered "The Father of American Intelligence and Special Operations." His Office of Strategic Services (OSS) was the precursor to the CIA.[1]

William J. Donovan passed away from a stroke on February 8, 1959, and was buried in Arlington National Cemetery. A life-size bronze statue of Donovan stands in the entrance lobby of the CIA's original headquarters in Langley, Virginia.[2]

In 2018 there were fewer than one hundred of the original Carpetbagger heroes remaining. Robert Eugene Holmstrom (seen here holding the Congressional Gold Medal) was one of them.

## 54

# A Personal Message from Robert Eugene Holmstrom

I N THOSE GREY DAYS WHEN THE United States of America was suddenly involved in World War II, men and women did what they were asked, and volunteered to do whatever was needed. It did not matter what branch of service you were in. There was never protesting by any civilian or military person.

In the military, no matter where we served in a foreign country there was a feeling of joy and relief when you returned to base camp and could see the American Flag flying overhead.

World War II was a monstrous brutality and was so viciously enacted in the course of those few years.

I was very proud to be with a group of men and women in the OSS, working in cooperation with British MI-5 Security Service and the SOE (Special Operations Executive), focused on covert operations and guerrilla warfare to shorten the war as much as possible.

If I could have a wish for peace in the world I would like to see all people treated equally regardless of race, creed or color.

*Robert Holmstrom*

# 55

# In Closing

A DEEP DEBT OF GRATITUDE IS OWED TO ALL of those who have joined the military, men and women alike, throughout our battles and wars and during times of peace as well. Their sacrifices are many and great.

This book focused upon one young man, who was chosen to become part of Operation Carpetbagger during World War II. Their missions were so dangerous and so covert that everyone involved was sworn to secrecy for forty years. Even after that many years passed, very little was spoken about it.

After more than seventy years since he took the oath, Robert Holmstrom revealed his life story and helped to lift the veil of secrecy about what some young American men and women were doing in war-torn countries abroad to protect our freedom.

*It has been a privilege and an honor to preserve the inspiring life story of Robert Eugene Holmstrom. He will now live forever in the hearts and minds of his family, his friends, those who read this book, and me personally.* —*Sandra Fabian Butalla*

The Holmstrom Family on the day Bob Holmstrom received the French Legion of Honor Medal, Jan.4, 2014. Back row (*left to right*): Amanda Davidson (Jennifer's daughter), Jennifer Nelson, Bob Holmstrom, and Nikki Klein (Jennifer's son's wife). Front (*left to right*): Rain, great-grandsons Henry and Riley Davidson, and Mark Klein (Jennifer's son).

# Appendixes
# A-L

*The following pages contain a variety of documents
including letters and photo images related to
Robert Holmstrom's life and military career.*

## Appendix A

### ARMY AIR FORCES

# Certificate of Appreciation

## FOR WAR SERVICE

TO

ROBERT E. HOLMSTROM

*I CANNOT meet you personally to thank you for a job well done; nor can I hope to put in written words the great hope I have for your success in future life.*

*Together we built the striking force that swept the Luftwaffe from the skies and broke the German power to resist. The total might of that striking force was then unleashed upon the Japanese. Although you no longer play an active military part, the contribution you made to the Air Forces was essential in making us the greatest team in the world.*

*The ties that bound us under stress of combat must not be broken in peacetime. Together we share the responsibility for guarding our country in the air. We who stay will never forget the part you have played while in uniform. We know you will continue to play a comparable role as a civilian. As our ways part, let me wish you God speed and the best of luck on your road in life. Our gratitude and respect go with you.*

COMMANDING GENERAL
ARMY AIR FORCES

Army Air Force Certificate of Appreciation

## Appendix B

ROBERT E HOLMSTROM

To you who answered the call of your country and served in its Armed Forces to bring about the total defeat of the enemy, I extend the heartfelt thanks of a grateful Nation. As one of the Nation's finest, you undertook the most severe task one can be called upon to perform. Because you demonstrated the fortitude, resourcefulness and calm judgment necessary to carry out that task, we now look to you for leadership and example in further exalting our country in peace.

*Harry Truman*

THE WHITE HOUSE

Thank You letter from President Harry Truman

# Appendix C

Liberté · Égalité · Fraternité
RÉPUBLIQUE FRANÇAISE

**CONSULAT GENERAL DE FRANCE
A
CHICAGO**

*LE CONSUL GENERAL*

Chicago, September 17th, 2013

Dear Mr. Holmstrom,

It is a great honor and privilege to present you with the Knight of the Legion of Honor medal. Through this award, the French government pays tribute to the soldiers who did so much for France and Western Europe. More than 65 years ago, you gave your youth to France and the French people. Many of your fellow soldiers did not return, but they remain in our hearts.

Thanks to the courage of these soldiers, to our American Friends and Allies, France has been living in peace for the past 6 decades. They saved us and we will never forget. I want you to know that for us, the French People, they are heroes. Gratitude and remembrance are forever in our souls.

To show our eternal gratitude, the government of the French Republic has decided to award you the Legion of Honor. Created by Napoleon, it is the highest honor that France can bestow upon those who have achieved remarkable deeds for France.

Thank you for what you did and congratulations,

Sincerely yours,

Graham PAUL
**Consul Général de France à Chicago**
205 North Michigan Ave-Suite 3700-CHICAGO IL 60601-Tel. (312)327-5200-Fax. (312)327-5201
contact@consulfrance-chicago.org

French Legion of Honor Medal and letter of presentation

# Appendix D

Bob's military jacket with a few of his medals and awards

## Appendix E

Assorted memorabilia, including a pouch for silk maps, compass buttons, tin container with matches and a striker top, 2 packages of chocolate, and a downward-facing flashlight

# Appendix F

Highly detailed silk map, designed to fold easily and fit in the small pouch

## Appendix G

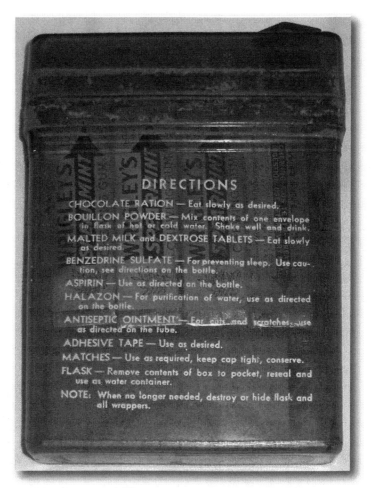

Emergency survival kit

## Appendix H

"Army Song Book"

# Appendix I

Assorted print memorabilia

# Appendix J

"In Case You Go Down" instruction cards in the event of a shoot-down and/or capture

## Appendix K

Military Awards Display Case created by Jennifer Nelson for her
father, Robert E. Holmstrom

## Appendix L

Congressional Gold Medal with names of OSS Groups, including the Carpetbaggers

# Chapter Notes

Chapter 1. ALONG THE SHORES OF GITCHE GUMEE

1. www.lakesuperior.com

Chapter 2. BETWEEN TWO WARS

1. www.history.com, "World War II."
2. www.history.state.gov/"Milestones/1921-1936/Kellogg."
3. www.history.state.gov, "Mukden Incident."
4. www.globalsecurity.org, "The Mukden Incident."
5. www.biography.com, "Benito Mussolini."
6. www.bbc.co.uk, "Divinity of Japanese Emperor."
7. www.biography.com, "Joseph Stalin."
8. www.biography.com, "Adolph Hitler."

Chapter 3. THE AMERICAN HOME FRONT

1. Persico, Joseph E. *Roosevelt's Secret War,* p.7.
2. www.biography.com, "Franklin D. Roosevelt."
3. www.thebalance.com, "U.S. Stock Market Crash of 1929."
4. www.U-S-history.com, "U.S. Stock Market Crash of 1929."
5. www.biography.com, "Franklin D. Roosevelt."
6. www.en.m.wikipedia.org, "William J. Donovan."
7. Ibid.

Chapter 4. CITY BOY

1. www.em.m.wikipedia.org, "Bronko Nagurski."

Chapter 5. BETWEEN THE ROCK AND THE HARD SPOT

1. www.edsitement.neh.gov, "From Neutrality to War."

Chapter 6. FDR TAKES ACTION

1. www.WW2pacific.com/prewar.html., "Pre-U.S. Entry to WWII."
2. www.warfarehistorynetwork.com, "The Norden Bombsight: Accurate Beyond Belief?"

3. Ibid.

4. www.atomic archive.com, "Manhattan Project."

Chapter 7. HELTER SKELTER

1. www.ww2pacific.com/prewar.html, "Pre-U.S. Entry to WWII."

Chapter 8. COUNTRY BOY

1. www.It.umn.edu, "Minnesota's Iron Range."

Chapter 9. BRITISH CODEBREAKERS

1. www.en.m.wikipedia.org, "Bletchley Park."

2. Ibid.

3. Ibid.

4. Ibid.

5. www.smh.com.au, "Enigma."

6. www.en.m.wikipedia.org., "Bletchley Park."

7. www.rutherfordjournal.com, "Father of the Modern Computer."

Chapter 10. FDR's SECRET WEAPON

1. Persico, Joseph E., *Roosevelt's Secret War*, p 17.

2. WW2pacific.com/prewar.html.

3. Persico, p.22-23.

4. www.warfarehistorynetwork.com., "William 'Wild Bill' Donovan: America's Spymaster in WWII."

5. Ibid.

6. Ibid.

Chapter 11. AMERICAN SPYCRAFT

1. Persico, Joseph E., *Roosevelt's Secret War*, p.81-90.

2. Ibid, p.90.

3. Ibid, p.94-5.

4. Waller, Douglas, *Wild Bill Donovan*, p.43.

5. Ibid.

6. Ibid, p.93-94.

7. Conant, Jennet, *A Covert Affair*, p.45).

8. Ibid, p.37.

Chapter 14. DONOVAN'S WEB OF ESPIONAGE

1. Waller, Douglas, *Wild Bill Donovan*, p. 96.

2. Ibid, p.113.

3. Ibid, p. 275-282.

4. Conant, Jennet, *A Covert Affair*, p.48.

5. Ibid, p.37.

6. Waller, p.101-102.

7. Ibid.

Chapter 15. CALL TO DUTY

1. www.google.com., "Number of Americans in WWII," wwIIfoundation.org.

2. www.google.com., "ww2historyinfo."

3. mn.gov, "USS *Ward* in WWII."

Chapter 16. TRAINING 101

1. www.thebalance.com, "Sheppard Air Force Base."

Chapter 17. IN THE CROSSHAIRS

1. www.en.m.wikipedia.org, "B-24."

Chapter 20. THE POT BOILS OVER

1. www.Britannica.com, "Bataan Death March."

2. www.historyplace.com/unitedstates/pacificwar/timeline.htm.

3. Ibid.

4. Ibid.

5. www.answers.com, "First U.S. troops in Europe in WWII."

6. www.en.m.wikipedia.org, "Battle of Midway."

Chapter 22. LAND HO!

1. www.en.m.wikipedia.org, "Firth of Clyde."

Chapter 23. THE FIRST FIVE

1. www.World Precision Instruments, wpiine.com "curette."

Chapter 25. SPIES, SUPPLIES, AND NOT JUST ANOTHER B-24

1. www.defensemedianetwork.com, "Carpetbaggers: Airmen of the OSS in Europe."

Chapter 28. A ROYAL TRIBUTE

1. www.en.m.wikipedia.org, "Queen Wilhelmena."

Chapter 35. BLANKETS AND BIRDS

1. en.m.wikipedia.org., "Battle of the Bulge."
2. Ibid.
3. www.americainwwII.com, "Pigeons in WWII."

Chapter 37. THE TIDE TURNS

1. Kindersley, Dorling, "Smithsonian WWII," DK Publishing, NY, 2015, p.334.
2. www.biography.com, "Benito Mussolini."
3. Ibid, "Adolph Hitler."
4. bbc.co.uk, "Joseph Stalin."
5. Ibid.
6. www.Britannica.com, "Hirohito."
7. Ibid.

Chapter 40. FINAL COUNTDOWN IN THE PACIFIC

1. www.lists.org, "Pacific Battles WWII."
2. www.historyplace.com, "World War II in the Pacific."
3. www.en.m.wikipedia.org, "Victory in Europe."
4. www.en.m.wikipedia.org, "Manhattan Project."
5. Ibid.
6. Ibid.
7. www.en.m.wikipedia.org, "Potsdam Declaration."
8. biography.com, "Hirohito."
9. en.m.wikipedia.org, "Hirohito."

Chapter 47. A VISION REALIZED

1. www.defensemedianetwork.com, "OSS."
2. Waller, Douglas, "Wild Bill Donovan," p.283.
3. www.biography.com, "Franklin D. Roosevelt."
4. www.en.m.wikipedia.org, "OSS."
5. CIA.gov, "History of the CIA."

6. Ibid.

7. Waller, Douglas, "Wild Bill Donovan," p.313-314.

## Chapter 51. CREATIVE DECEPTION

1. www.soldiers.dodlive.mil, "Strategic Trickery: the U.S. Army's Use of Tactical Deception.)

2. Ibid.

3. Ibid.

4. Waller, Douglas, "Wild Bill Donovan."

5. Ibid.

6. Ibid.

7. Ibid.

# Bibliography / Sources

The following books provided valuable resources for the historical portions of this book:

Conant, Jennet. *A Covert Affair*. New York: Simon and Schuster, 2011

Kindersley, Dorling. *Smithsonian WWII*. New York: DK Publishing, 2015.

McKay, Sinclair. *The Secret Lives of Codebreakers*. New York: Penguin Group, 2010.

Persico, Joseph E. *Roosevelt's Secret War*. New York: Random House Inc., 2001.

Waller, Douglas. *Wild Bill Donovan*. New York: Free Press, 2011.

Numerous websites provided additional historical information:
www.americainwwII
www.atomicarchive.com
www.bbc.com
www.biography.com
www.Britannica.com
www.cia.gov
www.defensemedianetwork.com
www.edsitement.neh.gov
www.en.m.wikipedia.org
www.Google.com
www.history.com
www.historylists.org

www.historyplace.com
www.history.state.gov
www.it.umn.edu
www.pimaair.org
www.smh.com.au
www.thebalance.com
www.wrfarehistorynetwork.com
www.WW2pacific.com

# About the Author

S. FABIAN BUTALLA WAS BORN AND RAISED in Toledo, Ohio, graduated from Bowling Green State University, taught junior high school English in Oregon, Ohio, and Los Angeles, California; senior high school English and College Writing at two schools in northern Minnesota; and then served as K-12 Media Director in five schools within the St. Louis County District of northern Minnesota, totaling more than thirty-two years in the field of education. She currently lives with her family in northern Minnesota.

# Discussion Questions

1. What hardships did Bob Holmstrom face throughout his childhood?

2. What hardships did you face in your childhood, and how did it break you or make you stronger?

3. Who were the people who had the strongest influences, both positive and negative, in Bob's life? Explain.

4. Who are the people who have had the greatest influence, both positive and negative, in your life? Explain.

5. How did Bob Holmstrom rise above the obstacles in his life to overcome them? Explain.

6. What actions could you take to overcome hardships or obstacles in your life, and who could help you?

7. After more than ninety years, what did Bob Holmstrom state that he valued most in life?

8. At this point in your life, what do you value most? Explain why.

*Also by S. Fabian Butalla*

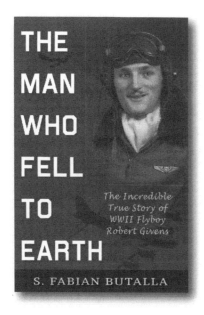

MEET ROBERT GIVENS…a young man, rejected by the Navy because he was colorblind, but who refused to give up his dream of flying. Against the odds, he became a B-17 top turret gunner with the United States Army Corps and was thrilled to be serving his country.

*The Man Who Fell to Earth* is the compelling true life story of a World War II airman, his harrowing fall from a B-17 as it broke apart over the North Sea, and the life he lived in the years that followed.

THE MAN WHO FELL TO EARTH
*The Incredible True Story of WWII Flyboy Robert Givens*
by S. Fabian Butalla

Available in paperback (ISBN: 978-1-55571-844-2)
and ebook (ISBN: 978-1-55571-845-9)

Available on Amazon.com and other online booksellers,
most bookstores or direct from Hellgate Press at
*www.hellgatepress.com*

Visit Us @

www.hellgatepress.com

www.palomabooks.com

Made in the USA
Lexington, KY
10 July 2018